EUROPEAN SECURITY IN A POST-BREXIT WORLD

BREXIT STUDIES SERIES

Series Editors: Alex De Ruyter, Jon Yorke and Haydn Davies, Centre for Brexit Studies, Birmingham City University, UK

With the vote on 23 June 2016 for the UK to leave the European Union, it has become imperative for individuals, business, government and the wider society to understand the implications of the referendum result. This series, published in collaboration with the Centre for Brexit Studies at Birmingham City University, UK, examines a broad sweep of topics related to Brexit. It aims to bring together academics from across the disciplines to confront and examine the challenges withdrawal from the EU brings. The series promotes rigorous engagement with the multifaceted aspects of both the 'leave' and 'remain' perspectives in order to enhance understanding of the consequences for the UK, and for its relationship with the wider world, of Brexit, and aims to suggest measures to counter the challenges faced.

Published Titles

Alex De Ruyter and Beverley Nielsen, *Brexit Negotiations after Article 50: Assessing Process, Progress and Impact*

David Hearne and Alex de Ruyter, *Regional Success after Brexit: The Need for New Measures*

Forthcoming Titles

Arantza Gomez Arana, *Brexit and Gibraltar: The Negotiations of a Historically Contentious Region*

PRAISE FOR *EUROPEAN SECURITY IN A POST-BREXIT WORLD*

'Superficially, Brexit looks quite straightforward; but, dig only a little deeper and the complexities are quickly evident. This is particularly so for the security sector. This book is an important and timely contribution to the debate and the need for specialists and wider public alike to have steady, informed hands guide them through the maze. The authors take the reader carefully through a phased introduction to these complexities and provide a detailed explanation of the respective legal and agency components of the intelligence/law enforcement sectors. One of the "stand-out" features of this book is that it is able to present the reader with a clear understanding in a straightforward and accessible reader-friendly style of what are highly complex, often highly nuanced elements'.

Professor Neil Renwick, Coventry University, UK

EUROPEAN SECURITY IN A POST-BREXIT WORLD

STEFANIA PALADINI
Birmingham City University, UK

AND

IGNAZIO CASTELLUCCI
University of Teramo, Italy

emerald
PUBLISHING

United Kingdom – North America – Japan – India
Malaysia – China

Emerald Publishing Limited
Howard House, Wagon Lane, Bingley BD16 1WA, UK

First edition 2019

Reprints and permissions service
Contact: permissions@emeraldinsight.com

British Library Cataloguing in Publication Data
A catalogue record for this book is available from the British Library

ISBN: 978-1-78769-840-6 (Print)
ISBN: 978-1-78769-837-6 (E-ISBN)
ISBN: 978-1-78769-839-0 (Epub)

Information and analyses included in this book are based on data as available as of July 2019.

Printed and bound by CPI Group (UK) Ltd, Croydon, CR0 4YY

ISOQAR certified Management System, awarded to Emerald for adherence to Environmental standard ISO 14001:2004.

ISOQAR REGISTERED
Certificate Number 1985
ISO 14001

INVESTOR IN PEOPLE

CONTENTS

LIST OF TABLES AND FIGURES

Tables

Figures

1

INTRODUCTION

1.1 INTELLIGENCE COOPERATION, INFORMATION SHARING AND LAW ENFORCEMENT IN A POST-BREXIT EUROPE

If the most of the major topics of discussion about Brexit are controversial and rich in contrasting views, only a few of them display the level of complexity found in the areas of security, here intended as including 'defence', 'intelligence' and 'law-enforcement'. Since the announcement of the referendum results in June 2016, the question that has occupied the most the political debate on European security is the one about the degree to which the UK is going to be damaged, if at all, by leaving the European Union (EU) and, therefore, what it carries in terms of participation to EU agencies and access rights to the existing legal, institutional framework and technical instruments.

This is well exemplified by two contrasting statements.

Sir David Omand, a former head of GCHQ, quoted in *Independence Daily*, declared that the UK will lose from Brexit.

> *We are part of an established information-sharing network with our partners whilst still retaining*

> *control of our border. The best of both worlds. Why jeopardise the flow of information we receive? (Omand, as quoted by Independence Daily, 16 April 2016).*

On the other hand, another senior intelligence officer, Sir Richard Dearlove, a former head of MI6, believes that Brexit would not damage the UK security. 'The truth about Brexit from a national security perspective is that the cost to Britain would be low', Dearlove says.

> *Brexit would bring two potentially important security gains: the ability to dump the European Convention on Human Rights – remember the difficulty of extraditing the extremist Abu Hamza of the Finsbury Park Mosque – and, more importantly, greater control over immigration from the European Union. (Dearlove, as quoted by Independence Daily, 16 April 2016).*

Both these statements are correct, and this should not come as a surprise, as they address two selected, different aspects of the security discourse. On the one hand, appreciation is shown for established networks and cooperative instruments that have proved to work remarkably well. On the other hand, a more traditional approach is displayed in relation to the needs of a sector – intelligence and national security – quintessentially sovereign and national, and still legally so according to article 4(2) of the Treaty on European Union (TEU): an area of international relations where integration tends to remain relatively low, although cooperation and information sharing do occur.

The old saying of intelligence that 'there are friendly countries, but do not exist friendly intelligence agencies' holds true even in present times. However, it is a fact that the EU's security as a whole strongly relies on the Member state(s)' willingness and capability to work together, share information and cooperate on issues of common interests – especially in counterterrorism and prevention of international crime. In this respect, the central role played by the UK, thus far, is also factually undeniable. There are no doubts that the EU security environment is going to change after Brexit: whilst the consequences are going to be particularly relevant for the UK, a certain impact will also be felt in the EU. The UK has always been one of the most important security providers at the EU level, and any post-Brexit arrangement will have to make sure this absence does not translate into an enhanced security issue for both sides.

It is conventional wisdom – a bit out-fashioned perhaps – that foreign policy, intelligence and external/military security are related to 'sovereign' activities; they are notionally quite clearly distinguishable from the areas of domestic security and law enforcement. So, it should be distinguishable, in parallel, 'military' matters and 'enemy' threats from 'police' matters and 'criminal' threats. Another clear distinction should be the one between 'national' interests and 'non-national' ones (including supranational, transnational and international). However, the times of such a clear-cut, 'Westphalian' simplified reading of the world are long gone. In the twenty-first century's global environment, the EU matters at large, and the very 'Brexit and security' discourses, seem to be overall characterised by fuzzier categories and multiple and diverse tensions.

Said tensions are generated by the interaction of different sets of old-fashioned polarities (foreign vs. domestic, enemy vs. criminal, etc.), in addition to emerging hybrid elements between 'classic' polar ones (most prominently, the hybrid threat of international terrorism, or that of transnational organised crime), all combining together in a complex picture with very little black or white elements, and certainly more than fifty shades of grey.

The EU institutional environment is also complex.

Several overlapping sets of EU-centred agencies and arrangements deal with security on the European continent, some including all the EU members, others that exclude some Member state(s) due to various opt-outs having been implemented (Denmark, Ireland and the UK, with respect to the Area of Freedom, Security and Justice). Finally, a few others do include third-party states due to specific arrangements between them and the EU (e.g. Norway, Switzerland, Iceland and Liechtenstein all participate in Schengen arrangements, including the Schengen Information System).

This has clearly been the result of a delicate balancing exercise conducted by 28 Member state(s), in addition to some non-members, to enjoy the benefits of cooperation without crossing some kind of individual, and domestically dictated, political and/or constitutional red line. The imperfect consistency of this complex system of sometimes seemingly overlapping arrangements and agencies is, thus, what, to some extent, made the system possible in the first place.

One of the obvious difficulties of integrating Member state(s)' national security and the EU apparatus lies indeed in the complexity of the EU structure. This has always been a well-known issue, complicated by the diverse characteristics and roles of the various EU agencies:

> *In the alphabet soup of bodies that you mention here, there is a slight mix-up between bodies which are essentially for policy formulation, like the terrorist working group and the counter-terrorism group, and the CTG, which has a much more operational structure.*[1]

As facts have proved, in the EU Member state(s), external terrorist threats and attacks (Madrid, 2004, London, 2006 and Paris, 2017) have worked as a collider, bridging external and internal security mechanisms and pushing strongly for enhanced information sharing and cross-country cooperation.

For what concerns criminal matters and law enforcement, the sector had first been reshaped in 1993 with the definition of the so-called 'Third Pillar', which included policies of police and judicial cooperation at the intergovernmental level amongst the Member state(s).

Later on, with the entry into force of the Lisbon Treaty, the 'Pillars' system has been superseded by an enhanced concept: that of 'Space', with an Area of Freedom, Security and Justice (AFSJ) offered by the Union to its citizens – as introduced in article 1(5) of the Amsterdam Treaty and later enshrined in article 3(2) TEU, and better specified in Title V (arts. 67 to 89) of the Treaty on the Functioning of the European Union (TFEU).

At the same time, some of the EU Member state(s) negotiated their limited or nil participation to the AFSJ, in consideration of their legal traditions and political and constitutional constraints: Denmark opted out of the Third Pillar under the Treaty of Amsterdam. A subsequent selective opt-in for Denmark in relation to specific measures in the AFSJ, negotiated along with the Treaty of Lisbon, has been rejected by Danish voters in a referendum held in December 2015.

Ireland and the UK negotiated opt-outs from the Justice and Home Affairs Council (JHA) under the Treaty of Amsterdam, subsequently transferred in the Treaty of Lisbon AFSJ, as defined in the Protocols attached to the TFEU. The option out has later been acted upon by the UK in July 2013, effective December 2014, before the entry into force of the European Court of Justice jurisdiction on matters related to Title V of the TFEU, with the subsequent re-opt-ins of the UK for selected arrangements of European cooperation related to the AFSJ.

Despite the mentioned opt-outs, the Lisbon impetus in developing the AFSJ had meant the EU reaching out for cooperation, approaching international organisations and third countries in the areas of security, law enforcement and justice – as it was often the case with EUROPOL's operations. Less-than-full access to facilities and benefits for non-participants to the AFSJ (whether EU Member state(s) or not) is made possible by special arrangements, bilateral schemes or access granted on a case-by-case basis option in for Ireland and the UK.

The aim of this short monograph is to explore what Brexit may possibly mean in terms of both the UK and European security, in the distinct albeit closely related fields of information sharing and intelligence cooperation, on one side, and law enforcement and crime prevention, on the other. Brexit consequences on either side of the Channel may probably not reach the same level of severity in those two fields, due to the quite different way the mechanics of cooperation work in the relevant areas – possibly causing a few problems in the latter, at least.

1.2. THE GENERAL CONTEXT OF EUROPEAN SECURITY. SHORT NOTES ON EUROPEAN DEFENCE COOPERATION

Before going into a detailed analysis of the subject of this study (internal security in terms of intelligence sharing and law enforcement across the EU), it is appropriate to offer a brief outlook of the overall EU security framework and the way it has been constructed over the decade. This is because, whilst not constituting itself an object of analysis, it provides the general context all security discourses in the EU, external and internal, have to come to terms with.

Any discussion of the European defence and general military security must start with NATO. This is because the NATO umbrella has historically been always present and relevant, for the non-EU countries (Iceland, Norway and Turkey) as well as for the EU ones, and for the UK as well. Even Denmark, who has kept self-exclusion from all EU military arrangements, has been a NATO member since its origin in 1949 – if, initially, in a formally limited one under the conditions of no NATO bases, no nuclear warheads and no NATO activities on the Danish soil.[2]

The Western European Union (WEU) was founded before NATO, in 1948 amongst France, the UK and Benelux countries, originally in a defensive key *vis-à-vis* a possible German resurgence, with a wide socio-cultural, economic and defence mission; it later reduced its scope of activities to common defence and economic matters only with the enlargement of 1954, when Germany and Italy were admitted. The WEU mission was then further reduced to defence matters only, as the EU and the Council of Europe eroded its original area of competence; Spain, Portugal (1990) and Greece (1995) later joined the alliance.[3]

Compared with the NATO, the WEU has been a much less dynamic international military organisation. An important political bridging role has been played by the WEU after 1954, through confidence-building cooperation and consultations in the area of armaments control, in the solution of the Saar issue, and eventually contributing to the admission of Germany in the NATO and to the UK's accession to the EU in 1973.[4]

After 1973, the WEU became more or less inoperative, as the Western European defence responsibilities were discharged by NATO, very much in line with the UK's traditional opposition to the developing of European autonomous defence capabilities.

Initiatives to reactivate the WEU were taken in the mid-1980s, in a fast-changing world setting, with WEU Conferences in Rome (1984) and The Hague (1987): fundamental principles have been established there on developing a European

Security and Defence Identity (ESDI), and enhanced security and defence roles of the WEU within, and identified with, the European Community and the coming EU, as the European pillar of the Atlantic Alliance.[5] The need to develop the ESDI within the NATO, with reinforcement of the trans-Atlantic link and full cooperation between NATO and the WEU was subsequently stated at the Ministerial Meeting of the North Atlantic Council of May–June 1996 in Berlin.[6]

The Treaty of Maastricht included the vision of European military institutions, and an obligation for Member state(s) of the EU to join the WEU, as part of this vision. A first Danish referendum after Maastricht returned a rejection of the Treaty, which compelled the EU to grant Denmark four opt-outs negotiated in 1992 at Edinburgh: from WEU membership, European Monetary Union, European citizenship and JHA/third pillar cooperative measures, before a second Danish referendum in 1993 permitted the ratification of the Treaty and, thus, its entry into force in the entire EU. The Danish exclusion from defence matters has later been confirmed with an opt-out in Protocol 22 to the Treaty of Amsterdam excluding the Danish Kingdom from the EU Common Security and Defence Policy.

The WEU, at its final stage, had a kernel of 10 NATO and EU Member state(s). Between 1992 and 1994, a number of non-EU NATO Member state(s) joined the WEU as Associate Members (Turkey, Iceland and Norway); a number of non-NATO, EU members did so as Observers (Austria, Ireland, Sweden and Finland), as well as Denmark, belonging both to the EU and NATO (but with an opt-out from the EU's Common Security and Defence Policy (CSDP)); and a number of non-NATO, non-EU became WEU's Associate Partners (Bulgaria, Romania, Slovakia, Slovenia and the Baltic States, which all eventually joined both NATO and the EU) – somehow reflecting the inclination (or necessity) of the EU towards including a high number of members accorded a wide range of statuses and options, rather than featuring a smaller club of member countries with a totally shared set of obligations.

The WEU did carry out a number of military or police or advisory missions – the first WEU forces having been deployed in the Middle East[7]; then most notably within Europe, in relation with political events in the Balkan area potentially affecting regional stability.[8] Its perceived failure in the Balkans, however, confirmed the need to further develop an adequate European security and defence capacity, lest maintaining the burden of European security entirely on the NATO and thus, significantly, on the United States.

In December 1998, the UK and France signed the historic St. Malo Declaration,[9] a purely bilateral document with a significant political impact for the EU, advocating the development of European defence capabilities, including autonomous EU military forces. This was one of the high points in UK's endeavours towards the development of a European defence framework leading to the following year's establishment of the EU's CSDP. This was followed in 1999 by the Helsinki Headline Goal and the Headline Goal 2010 (a document of 2004), two subsequent plans aiming at developing a substantial EU-controlled military force in line with the needs of the CSDP.

According to the Helsinki document of 1999, the EU should develop a force of 50–60,000 personnel, readily deployable to carry out the so-called Petersberg tasks: humanitarian and rescue tasks; conflict prevention and peace-keeping; combat in crisis management, including peace-making; joint disarmament operations; military advice and assistance; post-conflict stabilisation.[10] On the other hand, the subsequent 2010 Treaty between the UK and France was much more traditionally oriented, instead, towards bilateral military cooperation between the two signatory states, establishing a wide set of cooperative arrangements, including the creation of a Combined Joint Expeditionary Force deployable at short-notice.[11]

The WEU's eventual demise in 2011, as a consequence of the enhanced role of the EU in the area of security and defence hailing from the Treaty of Lisbon,[12] was accompanied by the absorption by the EU of some of the WEU's operational structures, most notably, the Institute for Security Studies and the Satellite Centre; previous WEU functions related to armaments cooperation and control have been transferred to the EU's European Defence Agency established in 2004.[13]

In 2016, the EU Global Strategy for the EU's foreign and security policy (EUGS) has been presented to the European Council in June 2016 by High Representative and Vice President of the Commission, Mogherini, followed by an Implementation Plan on Security and Defence,[14] devising implementing measures and action plans, and advocating a strong Permanent Structured Cooperation on security and defence (PESCO) based on articles 42(6), 46 and Prot. 10 TEU.

The development of an ambitious PESCO framework for cooperative projects and activities in the area of defence and security has been formally been given impulse between November and December 2017, with the participation of all EU countries except Denmark and the UK; a subsequent roadmap for its implementation has been adopted by the Council in March 2018.[15]

Whilst it is true that most of the defence cooperation in Europe still takes place under the NATO umbrella, things are changing fast after 70 years, due to the changed international setting. New scenarios include political westwards pressure from Russia (notably with the recent Crimean and Ukrainian crises) and China, and a number of different threats of other origins. A growing interest around European defence arrangements is detectable again, especially after the Trump administration's vocal stance on a relative disengagement of the US from Europe, coupled with repeated claims that contribution of resources for the functioning of the NATO should be rebalanced amongst the United States and its European partners. Brexit itself – both as an element of increased regional/global uncertainty and because of the loss of a traditional euro-sceptical EU partner – may contribute along with the other mentioned factors in reinforcing the European resolve towards developing its own fully-fledged defence and security apparatus.

Permanent EU forces would certainly represent a major innovation, compared to the traditional EU approach of deploying on-purpose contingents and task forces. One of such innovations certainly is the EU Battlegroups, tactical military units established in 2007, brought to operational readiness and never deployed thus far, with a view to fulfilling the tasks listed in article 43(1) TEU, and now also those included in the EUGS[16]: the initial difficulties preventing their employment are officially associated with difficulties in financing their functioning[17]; the issue of financial support for the Battlegroups has been addressed in 2015 with the creation of the Athena mechanism,[18] and is still being discussed with a view to further enhancing it.[19]

European cooperation in the area of security and defence is a complicate history, and an acronym-rich one. It had necessarily to be so, perhaps. Developing several threads to be connected in due course, to produce some kind of basic (thus far) fabric to work with was possibly the only way to achieve some result, in such a vital area for each of the EU Member state(s)-with lofty ideas expressed and reproduced often in different loci and documents, being accompanied by small, prudent implementing steps.

Much more could be added here for consideration. However, any in-depth discussions on EU defence would have led the present study away from the main focus of the analyses offered here – internal security and law enforcement rather than foreign security and policy – and have therefore been left apart for future research.

1.3. THE PRESENT WORK: FOCUS, APPROACH AND STRUCTURE

The limits of the present contribution are many, and most of them are self-evident: the first one is that it only considers intelligence sharing and cooperation arrangements, as well as law-enforcement institutions and normative schemes, almost without addressing the very important issue of the consequences of Brexit for European defence.

On the other side, security in the grey areas developing between the old-fashioned concepts of home affairs and foreign policy, in relation with hybrid threats – between military and police activities, combining the risks of both worlds – will be addressed, as falling within the scope of this work.

In methodological terms, this contribution discusses the present outlook building on the existing literature, and alternative outcomes of the current Brexit process with multiple scenario-analyses.

We also tried to streamline a most complex discourse, even though this has meant in some cases simplifying things more than we would have liked. It was a judgement call, as we assumed that any detailed analysis of the many ramifications of Brexit would not be possible at this stage beyond pure speculation.

The work is articulated as follows.

Chapter 2 will cover the legal basis of the EU security framework, discussing the basic texts of the EU that shaped it the way it stands today, including the founding provisions of the AFSJ and the rules on the EAW and EUROJUST. An important element of the European legal landscape, much relevant to our discourse, is the presence of the 1950 European Convention on Human Rights and the related European Court of Human Rights, and their peculiar relation with the EU law,

Courts and institutions. Chapter 2 will also examine possible legal shockwaves associated with the UK's legal system taking a diverging course with respect to the EU's, especially in the area of fundamental rights.

Chapter 3 will cover the EU's internal security landscape in structural terms, presenting in analytical terms the intelligence cooperation, information sharing, and law-enforcement supranational framework in the pre-Brexit era. The bulk of Chapter 3 describes the main actors in the field, both those formally established at a central EU level and the ones that are of more informal constitution – such as agencies collecting and sharing information at various titles both at intelligence and at law-enforcement levels, making the outlook particularly complex at times due to their duplicity of roles.

A short Chapter 4 will deal instead with the foreseeable consequences of Brexit in terms of internal security and discuss challenges (and opportunities) associated with possible different scenarios in the short and medium term, summarising analyses and findings.[20]

A final word about the sources used for research.

The authors have made use of the extensive document repositories existing on the EU web portal and the EU various agencies' ones, documents and discussions uploaded on the UK Government and Parliament websites, the academic literature on the topic in exams, and think-thanks. Other sources, especially for the official quotes, have been the national and international press and news agencies. Some internet sources have also been accessed, especially on EU institutions and related topics, which are remarkably accurate and well documented; references thereto proved effective as shortcuts to refer to the official documents abundantly cited therein.

All of the above are in the public domain.

NOTES

1. William Shapcott, former director of the Council Joint Situation Centre (SitCen), witness in: transcript of the UK House of Lords, 2, 4–66, 6 December 2010, online.

2. The three conditions have in fact been softened through decades, especially the first one, in relation to the territory of Greenland, made permanently available to US forces due to the strategic importance of its geographic position; and the third one. See 'Denmark' in the 'Origins: my country and Nato' section of the Nato webpage, https://www.nato.int/cps/en/natohq/declassified_162357.htm?selectedLocale=en. An embarrassing incident in January 1968 did strain US–Denmark relations, when it became public knowledge that a USAF B-52 crashed near the Thule Air Base was loaded with four nuclear warheads, thus violating the Danish nuclear-free policy.

3. See the 'History' section in the WEU webpage, still existing: http://www.weu.int.

4. As claimed in the 'History' section of the WEU webpage.

5. See Section 3, Reactivation of the WEU: From the Rome Declaration to The Hague Platform (1984–1989), in the 'History' section of the WEU webpage.

6. See the related Final Communiqué of 3 June 1996, available on the NATO website at https://www.nato.int/docu/pr/1996/p96-063e.htm. Accessed on 18 April 2019.

7. In the minesweeping Cleansweep operation in the Strait of Hormuz, 1987–1988.

8. 1993–1996: Sharp Guard naval mission in the Adriatic Sea, in cooperation with the NATO, and police and customs on the Danube river in cooperation with the OECD; 1995–1996, police activities in Mostar in cooperation with the local city administration established by the EU; missions in Albania (1997–2001), Kosovo (1998–1999) and Croatia (1999–2001). See the 'History' section in the WEU webpage.

9. Franco–British St. Malo Declaration of 4 December 1998, signed by French President Jacques Chirac and British Prime Minister Tony Blair, http://www.cvce.eu/obj/franco_british_st_malo_declaration_4_december_1998-en-f3cd16fb-fc37-4d52-936f-c8e9bc80f24f.html.

10. This is a list of duties for WEU forces included in the Petersberg Declaration, adopted by the Ministerial Council of the WEU at the Petersberg Hotel, near Bonn, in June 1992. https://eur-lex.europa.eu/summary/glossary/petersberg_tasks.html.

11. 'Treaty Between the United Kingdom of Great Britain and Northern Ireland and the French Republic for Defence and Security Co-operation', signed in London on 2 November 2010 between Prime Minister Cameron and President Sarkozy, in force since 1 July 2011.

12. Statement of the Presidency of the Permanent Council of the WEU of 31 March 2010, declaring the dissolution of the WEU having been decided by its contracting parties, in light of the WEU having accomplished its historical role, considering the Common Security and Defence Policy outlined in the EU Lisbon Treaty and the existence of the NATO.

13. See: eda.europa.eu.

14. Presented by the HRPV/Head of the EDA to the Council on 14 November 2016; https://eeas.europa.eu/sites/eeas/files/eugs_implementation_plan_st14392.en16_0.pdf

15. https://eeas.europa.eu/sites/eeas/files/pesco_factsheet_november_2018_en_0.pdf

16. EU Battlegroups Factsheet, on the EEAS page in the EU web portal, https://eeas.europa.eu/headquarters/headquarters-homepage_en/33557/EU%20Battlegroups.

17. EU Battlegroups Factsheet.

18. Council Decision 2015/528 of 27 March 2015, OJ L 84, 28 March 2015, 39.

19. EU Battlegroups Factsheet.

20. Although the work is a joint endeavour, Stefania Paladini authored Chapter 1 – Section 3; Chapter 3 – Sections 1,2,3,6 and 8; Chapter 4 – Section 3; and the Conclusions. Ignazio Castellucci authored Chapter 1 – Section 2; Chapter 2; Chapter 3 – Sections 4 and 7; and Chapter 4 – Sections 1, 2, 4 and 5. Section 1 of Chapter 1; Section 5 of Chapter 3; and Section 6 of Chapter 4 are a joint effort.

2

LEGAL FRAMEWORK OF EU SECURITY AND LAW ENFORCEMENT

As we write this chapter, the United Kingdom of Great Britain and Northern Ireland is still one of the 28 Member state(s) of the European Union (EU).

The 46-year-long (1973-2019) EU membership of the UK has brought about significant changes in the UK's internal legal landscape – not only due to the enforcement of the EU basic instruments but also due to the EU's day-to-day, current instruments and legislations. The UK's membership of the EU also produced the implementation in the Kingdom of a number of EU institutional and cooperative arrangements in several areas, including those related to security – in a two-pronged discourse, on law enforcement and justice, on one side, and on security and intelligence, on the other; in addition to grey areas in-between.

On the other side, the very EU law has acquired a specific flavour after the UK's accession in 1973, with the EU political, institutional, legal culture and output certainly being affected due to the influence acted upon by this new and large partner – including a typically Euro-sceptical national attitude, traditionally seeing Europe as a unified market only, whilst maintaining the UK's national, parliamentary sovereign prerogatives as much as possible, and reducing their integration in non-strictly economic matters.[1]

The legal and judicial framework relevant for security matters at EU level includes the Area of Freedom, Security and Justice (AFSJ); the Schengen Area; judicial cooperation agreements such as the European Arrest Warrant (EAW); EU prosecutorial entities such as EUROJUST and the recently established European Public Prosecutor's office (EPPO).

EUROPOL and other law enforcement and intelligence-sharing institutions and arrangements are dealt with in Chapter 3.

2.1. AREA OF FREEDOM, SECURITY AND JUSTICE

For what concerns criminal matters and law enforcement in the EU, the sector had first been shaped in 1993 with the definition of the so-called 'Third Pillar', which included policies of police and judicial cooperation at intergovernmental level amongst Member state(s). At a later stage, with the entry into force of the Lisbon Treaty, the 'Pillar' has been superseded by an enhanced concept: that of 'Space', with an AFSJ offered by the EU to its citizens – as introduced in Art. 1(5) of the Amsterdam Treaty, later enshrined in Art. 3(2) of the Treaty on European Union (TEU), and better specified in Title V (arts. 67–89) of the Treaty on the Functioning of the European Union (TFEU).

Title V features a set of general provisions devising an EU-wide space (arts. 67(1) and 68 TFEU) with no internal borders, common external ones, including common immigration and asylum policies (Art. 67(2) TFEU), and common internal security policies (Art. 67(3) TFEU).

General security strategies shall be made at the EU level (Art. 68 TFEU), with EU action to insure EU-wide internal security, coordination/cooperation amongst national authorities, approximation of national criminal laws (Art. 67(3) TFEU) – with national authorities maintaining their respective responsibilities (Art. 72 TFEU), under the principle of subsidiarity and proportionality (Art. 69 TFEU).

Title V also includes more specific sets of principles, policies, measures on asylum and immigration (Arts. 77–80 TFEU), judicial cooperation in civil (Art. 81 TFEU) and in criminal matters (arts. 82–86 TFEU); police cooperation (arts. 87–89 TFEU). The impetus underlying the vision in the Lisbon Treaty of the AFSJ also had the EU reaching out for cooperation with other international organisations and third countries in the area of security, law enforcement and justice.

At the same time, in consideration of domestic traditions, and political and constitutional constraints, Denmark, a Member state(s) participating in the Schengen Agreement, has negotiated not to participate in the AFSJ, confirming its previous exemption from the Third Pillar under a specific Protocol to the Treaty of Amsterdam.

A possibility was negotiated by Denmark along the Treaty of Lisbon to re-opt-in, similar to the flexibility offered to Ireland and the UK, in matters related to the AFSJ (Art. 7, Protocol 22 to the Treaty of Lisbon); this possibility, however, was rejected by Danish voters in a referendum in December 2015. Selected EU measures and rules related to the AFSJ are incorporated into the Danish legal system via intergovernmental arrangements between Denmark and all other relevant EU countries; a significant example of this is the Schengen *acquis* – its applicability in and to Denmark follows the operation of specific intergovernmental mechanisms between the Kingdom of Denmark and the rest of Schengen countries (Art. 4 Protocol 22 to the Lisbon Treaty) – which, by the bye, also include non-EU ones.

Ireland and the UK, also non-participants in the Schengen Agreement, negotiated an exemption from the EU law in Third Pillar matters at Amsterdam. Exemptions have been confirmed, with opt-ins, in the Lisbon Treaty in relation to selected measures of the AFSJ (Protocol 21 of the TFEU). The UK availed itself of this opt-in mechanism in relation to several measures, arrangements and institutions developed within the EU framework in relation with the AFSJ (e.g., the European Arrest Warrant (EAW)[2] or EUROPOL[3]).

Ireland also negotiated a standing full re-entry option (Art. 8, Protocol 22 to the TFEU), that is, an option to fully restore the applicability in the Republic of Ireland of Title V of the TFEU abandoning the entire exemption regime of protocol 21, simply based on an Irish government's request to that effect – an option that may at some point become expeditious to fully join the rest of the Schengen Area, should a hard land border eventually materialise between Ireland and the UK as an outcome of the Brexit process.

The UK also negotiated, in addition to the mentioned exemption from the AFSJ according to Protocol 22 of the TFEU, an option out from the enforceability of the EU Commission and of the Court of Justice of the European Union (CJEU) powers related to the AFSJ (Art. 10, Protocol 36 of the TFEU), associated with the end of the 5-year transition period, after the entry into force of the Treaty of Lisbon – that is, before 1 December 2014. Upon that date, the jurisdiction of the CJEU on the application of EU law in AFSJ-related matters would have become effective in the UK as well, unless that option had been exercised six months before the end of the transition period (Art. 10(4), Protocol 36 of the TFEU).

The UK did exercise the option, in July 2013. Article 10 of Protocol 36, however, includes a paragraph 10(5) affording the UK re-opt-in rights in relation to selected acts in the Schengen *acquis* – including an option to fully activate the powers of the Commission and the CJEU that have been opted out according to Art. 10(4), to permit the widest possible participation of the UK to the European *acquis* in the AFSJ.

2.2. SCHENGEN AND THE UK–IRISH COMMON TRAVEL AREA (CTA)

A most relevant theme associated with that of the AFSJ is the one of the Schengen *acquis*. The initial Schengen agreement is a non-EU international agreement signed in June 1985 by Germany, France and Benelux countries, to gradually grant free, unimpeded circulation of people by abolishing border controls amongst signatory states.[4] The treaty later developed into a Convention (1990, effective since 1995) for completely abolishing internal borders and developing common visa policies, thus creating a single area including signatory states, with a common system of external borders and border security.

The Schengen Convention was then adhered to by all remaining EU countries except Ireland and the UK, and eventually absorbed in the Treaty of Amsterdam of 1997 (effective since 1999) as a part of the EU *acquis* – with opt-outs for Ireland and the UK, and an obligation for all other EU Member state(s), including future new members, to eventually join the Schengen area as soon as practicable. The original Schengen Convention is, thus, no longer relevant as such since the Amsterdam Treaty, being instead relevant as a part of the EU law. Currently, all the EU countries except Ireland, the UK, Bulgaria, Romania, Cyprus and Croatia, are part of the Schengen Area – the latter four having an obligation to join it.

The then seven European Free Trade Agreement (EFTA) Member state(s) (including the then non-EU members Austria, Finland and Sweden) had collectively joined all the then EU

Member state(s) with an Agreement signed in Porto on 2 May 1992, effective 1 January 1994, establishing the European Economic Area (EEA)[5] – a common, barrier-free trade area devised to develop the idea of a common market space with the four liberties totally granted,[6] except for policies in the areas of agriculture and fisheries. The treaty has not been ratified by Switzerland, after a referendum in December 1992: this country participates in the free market area through (a high number of) specific bilateral agreements with the EU.

Rights of citizens of the EEA countries are those enshrined in the EEA Agreement, as well as in the EU Directive 2004/38/EC, also for citizens of non-EU EEA Member state(s). On the other side, EFTA countries shall adopt laws identical to the EU ones in the relevant common areas – the so-called 'mirror legislation' (Sevon, 1992, p. 334).[7] All legal differences between the EU and EFTA countries in relation to the interpretation or application of the EEA Agreement or in the areas where the law is identical on both sides[8] shall be resolved by the EEA Joint Committee, at political rather than legal level. Politically intractable issues may ultimately be referred to the CJEU, or subjected to arbitration (Sevon, 1992, p. 335).

Whilst Austria, Finland and Sweden eventually joined the EU, thus also joining the Schengen Area, extant non-EU members of the EFTA (Iceland, Norway, Liechtenstein and Switzerland) became part of the Schengen *acquis* due to individual arrangements with the EU. Said countries are also, thus, subject to amendments and further developments of the *acquis* within the EU legal system, with the only option of taking them as they are enacted, or leaving the entire Schengen Area arrangement – the reception of the EU *acquis*, the need of 'mirror legislation' and the ultimate jurisdiction of the CJEU on related issues could be a factor preventing a possible 'Norwegian' solution as a model for post-Brexit EU–UK long-term arrangements.

As seen, the Republic of Ireland and the UK are not parts of the Schengen Area. A different, Irish-UK CTA has been established as far back as 1923, soon after Irish independence – an *ante litteram* mini-Schengen of sorts for the British Isles, also including Man, Jersey and Guernsey.

The 1923 arrangement between the UK and the Irish Free State was not a legally binding instrument, rather being an informal agreement,[9] if ratified in both countries' subsequent legislation in 1925. The following arrangement between the two governments in 1952 (an official reference to a 'CTA' has first been made in the ensuing UK's *Aliens Order 1953*) was also a non-legally-binding one.[10]

The CTA has had its up-and-downs according to political circumstances through the twentieth century, marked by some more or less unilateral administrative or legislative steps taken by either country in response to actions of the other. Even recently, it has occasionally been suggested from both sides that some level of control could be reinstated.

A 2008 proposal of the UK Border Agency[11] suggested ID-checks at air and sea ports between Great Britain and (Northern) Ireland; and even of passport control between the UK and Ireland, with some kind of 'light control' of the Irish land border – with if still the absence of a permanent land hard border confirmed by both governments in a joint statement in 2008. The proposal was rejected in the House of Lords in 2009.

The two governments signed a Joint Statement in 2011[12] agreeing on measures to reinforce the security of the external borders of the CTA – an arrangement, again, with no legally binding nature, 'not intended to create legally binding obligations, nor to create or confer any right, privilege or benefit on any person or party, private or public'.[13]

This, however, neither mean that the issue has been settled, nor that a stable equilibrium has been found. After the Brexit referendum, a resurgence of discussion – especially in the

UK – can be noted with relation to preserving the CTA. Suggestions include, for example, permitting the maintaining of UK border checks at Irish ports/airports, allowing UK controls on non-EU and EU citizens (other than Irish ones) entering the CTA: the issue is very sensitive, and this proposal was not particularly welcomed by some Irish political quarters.[14]

Political statements from the Irish side, in relation to the implementation of the Schengen *acquis vis-à-vis* the enduring UK–Irish cooperation within the framework of the CTA arrangements, have been variable over time.[15]

In 2002, Ireland requested to fully participate in the Schengen arrangements, and its request has been accepted by the Council.[16] The Schengen *acquis* has not been implemented due to the unique Irish political history and circumstances and also following the Good Friday Agreement of 1998, to avoid a land border materialising again on the Irish soil, which could rapidly lead to an escalation of tensions – again detectable after the 2016 Brexit referendum, mostly at low intensity thus far, but also including some serious episodes.[17]

There is almost no need to mention how political and administrative arrangements such as the CTA, and/or institutional and legal schemes like the Schengen *acquis* have a strong security dimension. As a comparative remark, border security is doctrinally considered one of the pillars of internal security in the US, as per the Department of Home Security statement of mission: 'Missions include preventing terrorism and enhancing security; managing our borders; administering immigration laws; securing cyberspace; and ensuring disaster resilience'.[18]

Measures in a sophisticated set of cooperative border security arrangements may include authorising cross-border pursuit of suspects for police forces, of one state into the territory of another Member state(s); wider data exchange, not only in relation to border security and visa checks but also for law-enforcement purposes, as in the SIS-II development; management and protection of shared data.[19]

The Schengen system arrangements and *acquis*, however, did go further: border security responsibilities have been transferred from Member state(s)' responsibility to a complex system where the EU frontiers' security – along with related crime-fighting and intelligence activities – is in principle granted by the very Union, through its Border and Coast Guard Agency (FRONTEX) in addition to, and in cooperation with, the EU and non-EU individual Member state(s) of the Schengen Area.[20]

For a long time, the CTA and Schengen identified two separate areas of free movement of citizens, whereas the single market permitted unlimited internal circulation of goods in a larger area including both.

After Brexit, the CTA may still stand for the circulation of Irish and UK citizens (de Mars, Murray, O'Donoghue, & Warwick, 2018), if Irish obligations towards the EU and EU citizen's rights of free movement are not affected[21]; and if Dublin keeps its Schengen membership suspended.

However, and whatever the solution found for the movement of people, different economic policies between the EU and the UK if the latter leaves the common market and customs union would in principle require customs and excise controls established between the UK and the Republic of Ireland, both on land and at air/seaports.

Some major issues would arise, then. One is of an economic nature: for decades or centuries, the Irish economy has been integrated with that of the UK; a border would affect, in general, both countries' economies. But, especially, the Irish economy has become fully integrated between north and south after the Good Friday Agreements; a land border with customs and excise controls between the North and the South would produce acute unwelcome consequences especially in the North – particularly vulnerable as almost 60% of its £9.7 billion in exports of goods and services are bound to the EU, and some two-thirds of those to the Republic of Ireland (Biondi & Gonçalves Raposo, 2019; Mac Flynn, 2016, pp. 5–10); not to mention the impact of a hard border on complex manufacturing processes warranting a number of border-crossings steps, and on the life of some 23–30,000 cross-border commuting workers.[22]

Another issue would be of a more general nature, the Irish land border actually being one of the most sensitive issues associated with Brexit: the presence of a hard border on the Irish soil could have unforeseeable political consequences.[23]

With lingering memories of the Troubles that ended not so long ago (Larkin, 2019), a post-Good Friday, land border-free Ireland is a political achievement the stability of which is highly treasured by both London and Dublin, and by the EU.[24]

It must also be underlined how Northern Ireland, whilst being part of the UK, is constitutionally capable of joining the Southern Republic by referendum, as stipulated by the reformed Art. 3.1 of the Irish Constitution[25] as well as by Schedule 1 to the UK Northern Ireland Act 1998,[26] both enacted pursuing the Good Friday Agreement – the cornerstone of the northern Ireland constitutional uniqueness, in which both parties recognised the legitimacy of both Unionist and Republican political stances amongst Northern Irish citizens.

As a matter of fact, the 'Backstop' agreement between the UK and the EU reached in December 2017[27] provides for the absence of any hard border on the Irish soil after Brexit, and the continuing partial pertinence of Northern Ireland to the EU single market, as well as of the entire UK to the EU customs union, unless/until a trade and customs agreement is reached between the EU and the UK.

Should such an agreement not materialise, the UK may, of course, decide to leave the single market and the EU customs union; Northern Ireland, however, would still remain connected to both (and also become *de facto* part of the Schengen area, should the Republic of Ireland then implement its accession to it) as an effect of the Backstop – with a number of trade rules aligned to those of the EU and different from UK ones; and the consequent need to establish customs controls between Northern Ireland and the rest of the UK, also to be compliant with the UK's World Trade Organization (WTO)-related obligations, preventing the Kingdom from unilaterally opening the border with the EU unless also doing so with the entire WTO membership.[28]

An intra-Kingdom border in the Irish Sea, on the other side," would produce thorny political issues, *vis-à-vis* the expectations of Northern Irish Unionists, and the fundamental need of keeping the Kingdom a united one (Bridges, 2019; Kerr, 2019).

Removing/renegotiating the Backstop agreement will probably be one of the main concerns for the new government and Tory leadership, and also a major issue even within the very Tory party, after the demise of Ms. May's cabinet-to permit Northern Ireland to leave the single market and/or the entire UK to leave the customs union at any time, even through a 'hard-Brexit' option.[29]

However, some hard choice seems to be unavoidable in any case, between establishing a custom border on the Irish soil or in the Irish Sea. It will also be interesting to see how both parties will implement controls at the Anglo-Irish borders, including the land border or not, for non-Irish, non-UK–EU citizens crossing from Ireland into the UK.

2.3. BREXIT AND FUNDAMENTAL RIGHTS

One very important element of the legal landscape relevant to our discourse is the presence of a European Convention on

Human Rights (ECHR) and of a European Court of Human Rights (ECtHR) developed within the Council of Europe; and their peculiar relation with the EU law, Courts and institutions, increasingly involved in providing protection to fundamental rights. A brief description of the current, pre-Brexit legal framework is thus necessary.

The UK is a founding member of the Council of Europe, and a member to the ECHR signed in Rome in 1950. Its accession to the Convention dates as far back as 1951, well before the coming into existence of the EEC. Brexit, thus, will neither, *per se*, affect the UK's ECHR membership, nor will it affect the jurisdiction of the ECtHR and related case law.

The UK's Human Rights Act (HRA) 1998, a domestic enactment aimed at complying with obligations stemming from the UK's ECHR membership, should also remain applicable, unless amended or repealed.

The UK's ECHR membership implies the enforceability in the UK of general Convention's principles – with both the ECHR and the HRA construed according to the ECtHR quite liberal interpretive standards,[30] rather than to the more strict, literal and conservative common law approach (Hoffman & Rowe, 2010, p. 69 and ff. ones).

The EEC/EU relation with the ECHR has always been close. The Court of Justice of the European Communities (CJEC) has affirmed quite early the existence of basic human rights recognised in EEC Member state(s)' 'common constitutional traditions',[31] despite the absence of any related mention in the founding Treaty of the EEC.

Other decisions of the CJEC in the 1970s[32] expressly mentioned international treaties binding on EEC Member state(s) as sources of human rights to be protected at EEC level, including the ECHR (Groussot, 2006, p. 56; Schermers, 2000, p. 61).

An expanding protection of fundamental rights in the EEC/EU law and case law has been the result of a strong stance of the German Federal Constitutional Court, having first stated[33] that European Court's decisions could not prevent national top courts constitutional review until a protection of fundamental rights equivalent to the national one was fully implemented at EEC level, and later found[34] that such a level of protection had finally been achieved (Sirena, 2016, p. 119).

The Treaty of Lisbon of 13 December 2007 introduced a somehow problematic double standard protection of fundamental rights in the TEU: on one side, developing on previous CJEC and EU case law and further hardening its principles, providing that 'the Union shall accede to the European Convention for the Protection of Human Rights and Fundamental Freedoms', and that 'Fundamental rights, as guaranteed by the European Convention for the Protection of Human Rights and Fundamental Freedoms and as they result from the constitutional traditions common to the Member state(s), shall constitute general principles of the Union's law'[35]; and, on the other side, that the EU 'recognises the rights, liberties and principles set out in the Charter of Fundamental Rights of the European Union' (CFREU).[36]

The CFREU was first signed in Nice on 7 December 2000, as a political document without a legally binding character; it was later adapted in Strasbourg on 12 December 2007, the day before the signing of the Treaty of Lisbon to become a Charter 'which shall have the same legal value as the Treaties' with the entry into force of the Treaty.[37]

With Arts. 52 and 53 of the CFREU providing an alignment mechanism for Charter interpretation, to make it consistent with the ECHR, and, however, to guarantee an at least 'equivalent protection' of rights, it might seem that a perfect matching process of the EU and ECHR regimes has come full circle. This, however, is not the case.

The provision in Art. 6(2) TEU, according to which the EU should accede to the ECHR, has never been implemented, due to legal technical reasons – basically, to avoid EU acts and policies falling under the ECtHR's jurisdiction, with potential conflicts between EU policies and rules and the ECtHR[38]; meanwhile, impulse is being given within the EU institutions to press ahead the implementation of the CFREU.[39]

The two European systems of protection of human rights are obviously and formally intertwined, after the reception of the ECHR principles in the EU law – at least unilaterally, as the ECHR/ECtHR does not recognise the EU law in any formal way. Conflicts are reduced to the possible extent by the two European courts and EU national top ones, working in constant dialogue and learning from one another.[40]

However, potential contradictions between the two normative orders do exist, if for no other reason, for the very existence of two independent court systems dealing with similar issues (Sirena, 2016, p. 119) in different contexts. If, on one side, Arts. 52 and 53 of the CFREU provide for an at least 'equivalent protection' of rights between EU law and the ECHR, on the other side, a safeguard preventing such an alignment has been introduced by the CJEU in its first decision on Art. 53 of the CFREU, *Melloni c. Ministerio Fiscal*.[41]

The case, which may become very relevant for cooperation in law enforcement between the EU and post-Brexit UK, was related to the execution of an EAW following a trial *in absentia*. The CJEU held that rules agreed or consistently affirmed by EU Member state(s) (the Justice and Home Affairs Council (JHA) Framework Agreements, in this case) would have to be applied with preference to national standards – even should the latter be more favourable – if necessary to preserve the supremacy, unity and reliability of the EU law.

This decision contextualised, and effectively limited, the 'equivalent protection' principle stated in Art. 53 CFREU, with a view to preserving 'uniformity of the standard of protection of fundamental rights as defined in that framework decision', referring to the Framework decision 2009/299/JHA – the dis-application of which 'would undermine the principles of mutual trust and recognition which that decision purports to uphold and would, therefore, compromise the efficacy of that framework decision'.[42]

It may sound paradoxical that EU rules may enforce continental standards lower than some national ones, and still prevail over them. However, it must be considered that different solutions in fundamental rights protection, in such cases, are justified by the different approach of national constitutional rules, or of a general convention such as the ECHR – aimed at providing protection of basic rights in the very diversified context of the Council of Europe countries, *vis-à-vis* the specific context of EU countries; the latter featuring higher political, social, economic and rule-of-law standards; a high level of confidence amongst Member state(s); a significantly integrated EU legal landscape; and the importance and need of preserving this legal integration.[43]

On the other side, higher national protective standards of a EU Member state(s) may still be applied whenever they do not contradict the 'primacy, unity and effectiveness of the EU law',[44] to integrate areas of law not entirely regulated at EU level.

Going back to the UK and Brexit: the UK's legal system is characterised by the presence of internal legislation – the HRA 1998 – domestically implementing the ECHR, including the general principles enshrined in the Convention text and in ECtHR case law.[45] The system is also, generally speaking, tied with the EU law; which, in turn, on fundamental rights is significantly pegged – if partially – to the ECHR-based protective system.

It must be noted that the innovative role of the CFREU in the UK has been formally and substantially nil. The Charter itself expresses its nature of a restatement of rights already existing under the EU law or international law, or EU Member state(s)' national constitutional law and traditions.[46] A specific Protocol[47] to the Treaties, negotiated at Lisbon by the UK and Poland, provides that in those two EU Member state(s) the CFREU will not be introducing new justifiable rights in the law of the land,[48] with a specific express mention to reinforce the exclusion of the provision of Chapter IV on Social Rights.[49]

The Protocol further specifies that all references in the Charter to rights protected by national laws shall, for those two countries, be construed as strictly being related to their own national laws only (excluding thus, for instance, rules and principles developed within the common tradition of the EU Member state(s)).[50] A very recent European Parliament Resolution formally 'Regrets that to date, the Republic of Poland and the United Kingdom have not decided to withdraw from Protocol No. 30 of the Treaties'.[51]

In a post-Brexit scenario, thus, two immediate considerations are to be made in relation to this discourse.

First, the applicability in the UK of the ECHR and of the HRA will neither be brought to an end with Brexit, nor will cease the related jurisdiction of the ECtHR over the UK. Second, human rights-related external constraints for the UK will no longer come from EU law, rather being originated in the ECHR framework, its national implementing legislation, and related case laws.[52]

In this respect, the security objectives of 'scrapping the HRA'[53] are outside the scope of Brexit: the EU environment may prove a friendlier legal environment than the ECHR one for judicial cooperation and law-enforcement purposes, as demonstrated by *Melloni*.

However, in legal-historic and in political terms, the EU and ECHR mutually reinforce each other. Whether the ECHR in principle provides an original and higher level of protection of human rights, the EU provides a success story of implementation, and a different legal mechanism to protect the implementation of the ECHR. The two related courts established an intense judicial dialogue reflected in their case law (Cosio & Foglia, 2013; Spielmann, 2017). It is probably not incorrect to characterise European human rights law as a two-headed system, with a growing common body of principles and norms.

What is probably unpalatable for those in the UK adhering to traditional views on the relation between government and citizens, or aliens, is the occurred expansion – to some extent, a Germanisation[54] – of the EU fundamental rights discourse and legal framework. This character of the developing body of European fundamental rights law, associated to an approach rooted in continental law, is certainly unwelcome in the UK, due to its different (political and) legal tradition: broad and far-reaching constructive standards, and the very civilian idea of enforceable unwritten general principles of law are hard to digest for common lawyers. Moreover, the civil-law-like approach behind ECHR is also replicated, if in a hybrid form, in the very HRA 1998 (Art. 3).

If a full repeal of the HRA seems unlikely in the immediate future, it is reasonable to expect some divergence in the medium term between the related EU and UK laws, due to a substitution or partial amendments of the HRA, and/or to a simple repealing or amending of its Art. 3. And, however, to post-Brexit developments of UK case law, based on the application of traditional common law-interpretive standards rather than on continental law wider constructive principles. The Memorandum of the UK Government on Human Rights, 2018 offers a few hints in the sense.[55]

This transition will certainly be determined, co-determined, or to a significant extent facilitated, by the Brexit political process and momentum. Different standards of protection of fundamental rights may, in turn, affect the functionality of UK–EU judicial cooperation in the law-enforcement dimension.

2.4. HUMAN RIGHTS VERSUS SECURITY. A DIFFICULT TRADE-OFF

The liberty–security trade-off in public governance is at the crux of an open-ended debate (Baker, 2003; Blunkett, 2004; Dornan, 2011), not only in the UK. Two different polar models are determining an in-between spectrum of mixed epiphanies: a tight security approach, on one end, and a security model based on human right protection, on the other end. This is probably the conundrum any modern democracy has to confront at one moment or another, and the UK is no exception.

One may wonder how possibly a 'no-security' environment can produce security. This apparent paradox is based, more or less, on the idea that in a better 'rights' environment a number of incentives are diffusedly provided to avoid social deviance; and that in an enlarged pie of enjoyable rights, even an increase in deviant behaviour in absolute terms may still amount to a diminution in relative ones.

A EU-related case could be that of Baltic states and the way they deal with their large Russian minorities – an element of concern not only for internal security but also at a much larger geopolitical level: whilst a 'security' approach to the issue may lead governments to enforce restrictions for said minorities, a 'rights' approach may aim at fostering their integration and empowerment (Best, 2013; Włodarska-Frykowska, 2016), thus reducing the threat of them becoming cooperative or active parts of hybrid threats, attacks or warfare from Russia.[56]

Combining virtuously both approaches to maximise governance benefits can be a difficult exercise. Some suggest that game theory may provide a model for explaining how the exercise could be conducted successfully, thus increasing and optimising the liberty-and-security combination, shifting the related curve upwards in the liberty/security chart, and avoiding responses based on tightening security only at the expenses of rights, which may in some instances prove inefficient (Dragu, 2011). Most authors, however, agree on the existence in most cases of a liberty-versus-security trade-off (Gofas, 2012; Posner & Vermeule, 2007; Vermeule, 2011).

The two theoretical stances are not necessarily contradictory. Optimising liberty and security whilst trying to shift the entire curve upwards through long-term policy actions – a discourse which may either be banal, or extremely abstract and complex as in Dragu (2011) – is a different exercise from that of balancing them when actually having to work at the curve, in a historically given set of circumstances, especially in emergencies, when no mistakes will be forgiven: trading off liberties for security seems to be the quickest available and more popular response, whether the most rational/theoretically appropriate or not.

Historically, emergencies have been tackled by tightening security (of some, or of most) at the expenses of rights (often of some other) (Dornan, 2011; Silberstein, 2004; Walzer, 2006) – for example, with war tribunals to enforce military law, a classic example of this discourse; or with limitations of civil liberties to fight external or internal enemies, like with the USA's PATRIOT Act following 9/11.

Moreover, national circumstances may require political decisions conflicting locally with politically backed, widely accepted, or legally established EU notions: for example, the Italian approach to police investigations and criminal prosecution of terrorists during the 1970s, making ample recourse to dissociated terrorists granted a witness protection programme, in France was considered below the acceptable rule of law standards. The French position – a non-legal, purely political stance, the so-called Mitterrand doctrine, proclaimed by that French President in February 1985 (Ziccardi Capaldo, 2011) – prevented the French authorities in the 1980s from extraditing Italian suspects or convicted terrorists to Italy, for trial or enforcement of convictions.[57]

In this context, a post-Brexit UK may increase its internal security and try to re-introduce wider administrative discretion, when managing its own national security – for example, returning, perhaps partially, to the original common law principles on the non-judicially-reviewable nature of government acts, except in cases of extreme irrationality (as, typically, in the *Wednesbury* Court of Appeal case of 1947[58]).

In the specific area of judicial control over governmental action, very much related to the security discourse, post-HRA legal developments have introduced and consolidated also in the UK the legal notion of proportionality, of European/continental origin.[59]

It is seldom the case that a legal system undergoing significant changes can be totally reset to its previous state of affairs, after several decades since the new rules and practices have been established. The continental notion of proportionality has seeped in the UK legal system, including in some cases in areas not related to the ECHR[60]; in some other cases, it has been hybridised with the traditional common law notion of Wednesbury-unreasonableness, by expanding the latter substantially to the point of considering it as amounting to a (dis)proportionality test reasonableness including dimensions of weight and balance (Craig, 2013[61]) – if with a traditional common law flavour, using a structurally different legal reasoning to achieve a similar result (Feldman, 1999; Srirangam, 2016).

Other EU/ECHR legal principles are also ideal candidates to being softened in a post-Brexit UK, along with proportionality: administrative judicial accountability, procedural guarantees for accused persons and for petitioning citizens or aliens, social solidarity.

A corresponding reduction of these liberties and rights might possibly be perceived by many UK citizens as an acceptable price to pay, or maybe as (almost) no price at all, in exchange of a more secure environment, sacrificing procedural guarantees and benevolent governmental attitudes that the average British citizen feels not to be in need of. This would be perfectly acceptable in political terms, corresponding to different perceptions of rights and aspirations of the people of the UK with respect to those of the EU peoples.

The unexpected price, however, may come from the loss of (ease of) access to cooperative arrangements with EU – or ECHR – countries implying fundamental rights compliance according to EU or ECHR standards, and/or from higher transaction costs other things remaining equal (if possible, in the first place).

2.5 EUROPEAN ARREST WARRANT (EAW)

The EAW came at the end of a long convergence of European legal systems in this area of cooperation, with a number of bilateral or multilateral instruments enacted amongst European States since the European Convention on Extradition of 1957, progressively reducing frictions and imperfect carriages of justice. A 2002 Council Decision set the principles of a new EU cooperative model, to be implemented by all Member state(s)' legislation.[62]

The UK, whilst having opted out of the EU ASFJ in 2013, negotiated to maintain its participation in this particular instrument.[63]

The core idea at the foundations of the EAW is that of having cross-border judicial cooperation working in a mode different from the previous state of affairs, based on old concepts of national sovereignty, and on judicial assistance obtained through diplomatic channels. The new model moves cooperation much forward, from a 'diplomatic cooperation' to a 'direct enforcement' model: in other words, from politics to law, giving full effect to the principle of mutual recognition of judicial decisions amongst EU Member state(s), with a limited number of exceptions/exemptions/conditions.

According to the EAW scheme, an arrest requested by a competent authority in an EU country shall be executed by the judicial authorities of a different one, for the purpose of enforcing a custodial order or a conviction, with the entire process developing at purely judicial level.[64] The Commission published an EAW Handbook to assist judicial authorities in the discharge of their related duties, including guidelines and discussions of important major case law of the CJEU interpreting the framework decision on EAW, periodically reviewed.[65]

Some basic conditions shall be met for the EAW mechanism to be operational: a conviction must be one of an at least four months' prison term, whilst a custodial order must be related to a crime punished with a maximum prison term of at least one year.[66] Moreover, there is no 'double criminality' requirement – that is, the act committed must not necessarily qualify as criminal in both countries – for a number of specifically offences punishable in the requesting country with a maximum prison term of at least three years.[67]

The measures are applicable even for an EAW issued against a citizen of the required state, to be prosecuted in the requiring state – a very significant innovation, due to the traditional and quite common approach of national legal systems towards protecting their own nationals refusing to surrender them to a third country.[68] A previous, quite unusual similar arrangement, amongst a much smaller number of socially and legally much more homogenous countries, was that amongst Nordic ones (Mathisen, 2010, p. 10).

Execution of an EAW shall be refused in few cases, listed in Art. 3 of the Framework Decision of 2002, including *bis in idem* or double jeopardy, executions against minors, cases covered by an amnesty in the requested country. In other cases, the refusal is discretional, mostly in association with actual, possible, or past double prosecutions, offences time-barred in the requested country, or other jurisdictional conflicts.[69]

Fundamental-rights-related conditions are included in the foundations of the EAW system, the lack of which may amount to a sufficient ground of refusal of execution. Despite infringement of fundamental rights not being expressly included in the list of grounds for refusal, as per Art. 3, Recitals 12 and 13 in the Preamble and Art. 1(3) of the Framework Decision do include fundamental rights considerations in the assessment grounding the required state's decision on a request of execution of a EAW: proportionality shall be found between the fact and the measure; due process principles in the requesting state shall have been complied with; EU fundamental rights of the relevant person shall not be endangered as a possible consequence of the measure requested.[70]

At least two thorny issues may, thus, emerge in post-Brexit UK.

The first one is in the fact that only the EU dimension of the EAW permitted overcoming the traditional, legal and constitutional constraints preventing most states to surrender their own nationals to the authorities of a foreign country – the EU having become a part of Member state(s)' national constitutional architecture after Maastricht and Lisbon, thus no longer being (entirely) foreign for these purposes.

As a matter of fact, on 17 February 2019, Germany – who had amended its Constitution to permit the EAW mechanism, maintaining its prohibition of surrender of own nationals to non-EU countries – notified the Council that it would no longer surrender any German national to any UK authorities immediately after Brexit, irrespective of Brexit occurring in a 'deal' or 'no-deal mode'.[71]

This kind of constitutional or legal constraints, preventing surrender/extradition of an own citizen to the authorities of another (non-EU) requesting state is also present in most other EU countries. A report of the Home Affairs Committee of the House of Commons on UK–EU Security Cooperation after Brexit underlined, in relation to the EAW, that

> *It is imperative that the UK's future relationship with the EU includes speedy and simple extradition arrangements for serious crime, based on mutual recognition of judicial decisions, and that these arrangements are as similar as possible to the EAW model. In particular, being forced to fall back on the 1957 European Convention on Extradition would be a catastrophic outcome.*[72]

A second serious issue for the UK after Brexit will be the fundamental rights one, as soon as its legal system will start diverging significantly from the related European standards of protection – the divergence potentially being ground for refusal of an EU Member state(s) to surrender an individual to the UK authorities.

2.6 EUROJUST

EUROJUST has been established with Council Decision no. 2002/187/JHA, amended by Council Decision no. 2003/659/

JHA, as a coordinating agency for national prosecution services of EU Member state(s). One Representative, one or more Deputies and one or more Assistants for each EU Member state(s) (Prosecutors, Judges or Police Officers) are based at the EUROJUST headquarters in The Hague.

The mission of EUROJUST originally included cooperation and liaising with EUROPOL, OLAF, INTCEN, FRONTEX and any other EU agency, national prosecutorial authorities[73] and the European Judicial Network.[74] Other competences included assisting national authorities in cross-jurisdictional matters, including EAWs, and all requests of judicial assistance amongst judicial authorities of Member state(s); as well as that of assisting mixed investigation teams assembled within the framework of prosecutorial cooperation.[75]

Prosecution services in the EU Member state(s) remain within each Member state(s) sphere of responsibility, being one of those basic functions of the state traditionally closely associated with the core of sovereignty. They are also part, in a stricter or wider sense, of each state's judiciary apparatus, thus representing one of the three fundamental powers of the state in Montesquieu's vision, at the basis of Western rule of law and institutions.

On the other side, in a EU characterised by the so-called Four Freedoms, that is, absence of internal borders, European citizenship, and a common AFSJ, a plausible ultimate vision could be that of developing a full set of EU state-like basic functions, working along with Member state(s)' ones – including legislature, government, judiciary and prosecution, defence, border security and internal police forces.

In any case, even in shorter term and/or in a less ambitious European vision, close cooperation and effective coordination amongst national prosecution services are critical for the common AFSJ, *vis-à-vis* the challenges posed by transnational criminality.

As a comparative remark, the Italian model of mafia-related prosecution, having effectively fought organised crime for decades (Paoli, 2007), developed its very specific traits and legal framework starting in the 1980s precisely with the intuition of Judge Giovanni Falcone that prosecution and investigations against organised crime needed to be coordinated at a higher-than-local level to be effective. This vision had initially been opposed at various levels, including by large segments of the judiciary concerned with governmental interference and general rule of law issues, before becoming accepted and fully implemented with a wide array of legal instruments (La Spina, 2014; Nanula, 2009; Paoli, 2007; Sergi, 2013, 2017, p. 61 and ff. ones).[76]

Council Decision 2009/426/JHA enhanced EUROJUST's strength, introducing a round-the-clock On-Call Coordination arrangement to deal with coordination activities urgently required, and expanded EUROJUST's competences to include all crimes and offences for which EUROPOL is competent to act,[77] including 'serious crime affecting two or more Member state(s), terrorism and forms of crime which affect a common interest covered by a Union policy, as listed in Annex I', and crimes related to those.[78] Annex I of the EUROPOL Regulation (EU) 2016/794 features a list of 30 categories of serious offences.[79]

Priorities determined by the Council in EUROJUST's current agenda include terrorism, human trafficking, fraud, corruption, IT crimes, money-laundering and organised crime in various sectors of the economy. With a staff of about 260, EUROJUST conducts some 200 operational meetings per year, dealing with some 2,000 cases per year.[80]

National members of EUROJUST, initially discharging coordination and facilitation duties, received much increased operational powers with Council Decision 2009/426/JHA, including powers – to be enacted in agreement with their national authority – to issue requests and decisions on judicial cooperation, execute such decisions and order investigative measures established within the framework of coordination meetings, for example, to conduct simultaneous arrests – as well as more limited urgency powers to act directly, such as those to authorise and coordinate controlled deliveries in their Member state(s) and executing requests and orders in matters of judicial cooperation.[81] National members of EUROJUST are free to exchange amongst them any information necessary to discharge EUROPOL's duties,[82] at the same time being bound by EU security standards in managing EU-classified information.[83]

Finally, EUROJUST has the mandate of establishing cooperation agreements with non-EU authorities: Liaison Officers from Norway and the US are based in The Hague, thus far. A Representative from the UK may be the next third-party Liaison Officer, quite obviously. Since Council Decision 2009/426/JHA EUROPOL also has the authority to second Officers or Magistrates to third countries.[84]

A Regulation has been enacted in late 2017, consolidating and innovating EUROJUST afresh, in its entirety, since 12 December 2019.[85] The reasons for this new instrument are stated in its initial Recitals: compliance with the TFEU providing for EUROJUST functioning to be disciplined by this type of instrument and need to provide normative clarity, thus repealing previous Council Decisions; strengthening the administrative dimension of EUROJUST; regulating data protection according to the general EU Regulation 2018/1727.

A specific new set of provisions is regulating the allocation of responsibilities between EUROJUST and EPPO: Regulation 2018/1727 establishes the competence of EUROJUST for all offences for which EPPO is competent, in all cases when EPPO may not act directly due to the inapplicability of the EPPO Enhanced Cooperation framework – that is, when the relevant cooperation involves Ireland, Denmark, the UK or a third country: in these cases, EU Member state(s), or the very EPPO, may activate cooperation within the wider EUROJUST framework.[86]

2.7. EUROPEAN PUBLIC PROSECUTOR'S OFFICE (EPPO)

A EPPO 'established from EUROJUST' (Art. 86(1) TFEU) has been devised in the Lisbon Treaty to investigate and prosecute, together with EUROPOL (Art. 86(2) TFEU), crimes against the financial interests of the EU before the competent national criminal courts (Art. 86(2) TFEU)[87] – completing the EUROJUST list of duties and the EUROPOL-EUROJUST investigative continuum with the possibility of directly bringing court actions before national courts, thus stepping up the process of developing a full set of EU inherent state-like functions. The creation of the EPPO has been proposed by the Commission in 2013 – with an opt-out from it for Denmark, Ireland and the UK – and developed under enhanced cooperation amongst initially 20, now 22, EU Member state(s). The EPPO should become active at the end of 2020, with a centralised Office and European Prosecutor's Delegates in each Member state(s).[88]

This new EU institution will contribute to the development of the AFSJ, at law-enforcement level and also improving the overall circulation at European level of security-relevant information. If, on one side, its original specific focus on EU frauds will probably make it seem less immediately relevant for the general security of and in the EU, and not relevant for the UK, on the other side the EPPO activities will also contribute to developing a Europe-wide professional expertise and knowledge in the wider area of transnational financial crime.

Organised criminals and terrorists need to raise funds, and to use them to procure whatever they need to be operational: developing and sharing EU-wide expertise in dealing with financial, tax, internet crime will be critical for the security needs of the twenty-first century (Kendall, 2004; Nguyen, 2017; Ryder, 2017; Scanlan, 2004).

Legal reality as well as legal history teach well how important it is to develop the ability to track financial resources and financial and taxation law violations, to eventually reach, indict, and convict members of large criminal and terrorist organisations. The US war on terror also included a fundamental financial dimension, as it is clear from the very PATRIOT Act 2001, providing measures to contrast illegal financial transactions including in third-party states.[89] There are some egregious, well-known cases of transnational enforcement of the Act, such as that against Banco Delta Asia-a Chinese bank from Macau involved in illegal financial transactions for the benefit of the North Korean government-targeted in 2005 by the US Treasury with an order according to Section 311 of the Act to all US business and financial entities, to interrupt any business activity with that bank.[90]

Back in time, the FBI's successful arrest of the infamous Chicago gangster Al Capone in 1931 was made possible by following the threads of his income tax frauds and enforcing the federal taxation criminal law to have him, in the event, serve a term in jail.[91]

On the European continent, again the Italian long experience in fighting terrorism and organised crime offers a comparative example also in this respect. *Guardia di Finanza*, the Italian financial military police – established in 1862 as the Italy's customs and excise police – is very active in contrasting domestic and international organised crime. It can operate in a military, internal security and intelligence mode; or in a judicial police mode, making extensive use of its very specific expertise and operational culture[92] when cooperating with the Italian specialised anti-mafia prosecution service, and/or with other prosecutors enforcing financial and other white-collar criminal laws.

This seems to be at the basis of the Commission's initiative of September 2018, under the auspices of Jean-Claude Juncker, in order to expand the competences of the EPPO to include prosecuting cross-border terrorist activities. Whether desirable or not, this would be legally feasible, according to the EU law, as the TFEU allows entrusting the EPPO with the prosecution of serious transnational crimes.[93]

It is perhaps reasonable to foresee proposals coming, at some stage in the future, to progressively enlarge the scope of law-enforcement activities of the EPPO, towards matching in principle the entire range of EUROJUST and EUROPOL activities: a trend is detectable in the more recent EU legal reforms towards aligning, consolidating, strengthening and coordinating institutions and normative instruments related to the AFSJ.

The UK's initial opt-out from the EPPO and the AFSJ, and now Brexit, in principle should permanently prevent the UK from accessing the EUROPOL-EUROJUST-EPPO cooperation, as a whole, without any extant re-opt-in for any of the related arrangements. However, the cooperative arrangements already in place with respect to EUROPOL may still be confirmed at UK–EU negotiation level; or new arrangements may be worked out – individually or as a package within the framework of a UK–EU Brexit long-term deal. Whilst the EPPO would certainly remain irrelevant for a post-Brexit UK, the EUROJUST cooperation may not be lost, by establishing a EUROJUST third country cooperative link, such as those already in place with Norway and the US.

NOTES

1. A typically UK description of the EU is this one: 'The European Union (EU) consists of 28 Member state(s), including the UK .... The EU was set up first and foremost to make it easier to sell goods, to work and to conduct other forms of business between the participating countries. Whilst human rights protections were not originally parts of this system ... EU law now contains a number of citizenship rights and human rights derived from different sources' – taken from the webpage of 'The UK in a Changing Europe', an academic initiative researching Brexit and UK–EU issues. https://ukandeu.ac.uk/fact-figures/whats-the-difference-between-th... european-court-of-human-rights-and-the-european-court-of-justice/.

2. See below, Section 2.5.

3. See below, Chapter 3, Section 3.3.

4. 'Agreement between the Governments of the States of the Benelux Economic Union, the Federal Republic of Germany and the French Republic on the gradual abolition of checks at their common borders', *43 OJ of the EU, L 239, 22.9.2000, 13–18, www.eur-lex.europa.eu.*

5. Agreement on the European Economic Area, *Official Journal L 001, 03/01/1994 P. 0003–0036.*

6. European Parliament, Briefing No. 32, The European Economic Area (EEA) and the enlargement of the European Union, 1998. Retrieved from http://www.europarl.europa.eu/enlargement/briefings/32a2_en.htm.

7. According to the EEA Agreement, the EEA features an EEA Council and an EEA Joint Committee, dealing with common matters between the EU and the EFTA and their respective Member state(s).

8. EEA Agreement, Art. 111.

9. The Irish State was still considered part of the UK for immigration purposes in the *Aliens Order 1923* (UK).

10. CTA internet source. Accessed on 10 April 2019.

11. UK Home Office, Border Agency Consultation Paper of 24 July 2008, proposed by Liam Byrne, then Minister of State for Borders and Immigration.

12. 'Joint Statement Regarding Co-Operation on Measures to Secure the External Common Travel Area Border', signed on 20 December 2011, by the Irish Minister of Justice and the UK's Minister of Immigration.

13. Joint Statement, Article 8.

14. A short account of discussion and media news with respect to that is in Wikipedia, CTA. Accessed on 10 April 2019.

15. Political statements and other media information available on internet, Wikipedia-Opt-outs in the European Union. Accessed on 10 April 2019.

16. Council Decision (2002/192/EC) of 28 February 2002 on Ireland's request to take part in some of the provisions of the Schengen acquis; *OJ L 64*, 7 March 2002, 20.

17. An incident in Derry/Londonderry on 18 April 2019, Good Friday's eve, resulted in the shooting and death of Irish journalist Lyra McKee, during riots exploded following weeks of growing political tension. A formation named 'New IRA' took responsibility for the killing, stating it has been a mistake and offering apologies to the journalist's family and friends.

18. See the DHS website, https://www.dhs.gov/mission. McGlynn & Garner refer to the DHS mission as a simplified three-pillar one: customs and border security, counterterrorism and disaster resilience (McGlynn & Garner, 2019, p. xiv).

19. Below, Chapter 3, Section 3.5.

20. Below, Chapter 3, Section 3.4.

21. Joint Report of Negotiators of the EU and UK Government of December 2017, para. 54; wording to the same effect have also been inserted by the EU commission in the Draft Withdrawal Agreement of March 2018, at 110.

22. House of Commons, Northern Ireland Affairs Committee (2018, p. 7), making reference to the Centre for Cross-Border Studies' estimates.

23. House of Commons, Northern Ireland Affairs Committee (2018, pp. 7–8).

24. House of Commons, Northern Ireland Affairs Committee (2018, p. 7).

25. '[...] a united Ireland shall be brought about only by peaceful means with the consent of a majority of the people, democratically expressed, in both jurisdictions in the island', repealing the set of norms regulated by Articles 2 and 3 of the Constitution in their previous version, in which a territorial claim was made by the Republic of Ireland to 'the national territory [consisting] of the whole Island of Ireland...' (text of old Art. 2)

26. Providing that the Secretary of State for Northern Ireland shall hold a referendum 'if at any time it appears likely to him that a majority of those voting would express a wish that Northern Ireland should cease to be part of the United Kingdom and form part of a united Ireland'.

27. Joint Report of Negotiators of the EU and UK Government of December 2017, paragraphs 43, 45, 49, 50 and 51.

28. House of Commons, Northern Ireland Affairs Committee (2018, p. 26).

29. All Tory candidates (including frontrunners B. Johnson and J. Hunt) to the leadership of the Conservative Party and, after her resignation (May 2019), to replacing Ms. May as the Prime Minister of the UK in July 2019, have been vocal in promising such a renegotiation of the Backstop agreement.

30. Human Rights Act 1998, Section 3(1).

31. CJEC, 17 December 1970, C-11/70, *Internationale Handgesellschaft mbH* v. *Einfuhr- und Vorrastelle fur getreide und Futtermittel*; European Court Reports, 1970, 01125.

32. CJEC, 14 May 1974, C-4/73, *Nold* v. *European Commission,* European Court Reports 1974, 00491; 28 October 1975, C-36/75, *Rutili c. Ministre de l'Intérieur*, European Court Reports 1975, 01219; 13 December 1979, C-44/79, *Hauer* v. *Land Rheinland-Pfalz*, European Court Reports 1979, 03727.

33. *Bunderverfassungsgericht*, 29 May 1974, *Solange I*, in BverfGE 37, 271, later becoming one of the foundational elements of the

theory of national counter limitations to the national cession of sovereignty to European institutions (Tesauro, 2013, p. 11).

34. *Bunderverfassungsgericht*, 22 October 1986, *Solange II*, in BverfGE 73, 339; and 12 October 1993, *Maastricht*, BverfGE 89, 155.

35. Art. 6(2) and (3) TEU.

36. Art. 6(1) TEU.

37. Art. 6(1) TEU.

38. A more detailed explanation of the reasons behind the delay – or avoidance, thus far – in implementing Art. 6(2) TEU with the full accession of the EU to the ECHR is given in the 'Legislative Train Schedule' titled 'Completion of accession of the EU to the ECHR' published on the website of the European parliament, http://www.europarl.europa.eu/legislative-train/theme-area-of-justice-and-fundamental-rights/file-completion-of-eu-accession-to-the-echr

39. European Parliament resolution of 12 February 2019, on the implementation of the Charter of Fundamental Rights of the European Union in the EU institutional framework, http://www.europarl.europa.eu/doceo/document/TA-8-2019-0079_EN.html

40. 'Dialogue' is in fact one of the most used terms to indicate the existing cooperation between the two European courts, and amongst them and European Member state(s)' top courts. See, for example, the very title of Cosio and Foglia (2013).

41. CJEU, 26 February 2013, C-399/11, *Melloni* v. *Ministerio Fiscal*, ECLI:EU:C:2013:107; discussed below, Section 1.5.

42. *Melloni*, 63. Also see the Opinion of Advocate General Bot delivered on 2 October 2012 in the same case, ECLI:EU:C:2012:600, especially at 99–111, and the literature cited there in by Mr. Bot (Arroyo Jiménez, 2011; Tinsley, 2012, p. 28; Van De Heyning, 2011; Widmann, 2002, p. 353). Also see Alkema, van der Hulle, and van der Hulle (2015).

43. See the Opinion of Advocate General Bot delivered on 2 October 2012 in *Melloni*, ECLI:EU:C:2012:600, especially at 99–111.

44. CJEU, 26 February 2013, *Åklagaren* v. *Åkerberg Fransson*, C-617/10, ECLI:EU:C:2013:105, 29; this decision has been issued on the same day as *Melloni*. In the same line, CJEU, 30 May 2013, *Jeremy F.* v. *Premier Ministre*, C-168/13 PPU, ECLI:EU:C:2013:358.

45. Human Rights Act 1998, Section 3(1).

46. 'This Charter reaffirms, with due regard for the powers and tasks of the Community and the Union and the principle of subsidiarity, the rights as they result, in particular, from the constitutional traditions and international obligations common to the Member state(s), the Treaty on European Union, the Community Treaties, the European Convention for the Protection of Human Rights and Fundamental Freedoms, the Social Charters adopted by the Community and by the Council of Europe and the case-law of the Court of Justice of the European Communities and of the European Court of Human Rights'. – CFREU, Preamble. Also see the European Union (Withdrawal) Bill – European Convention on Human Rights – Memorandum by the Department for Exiting the European Union of 18 January 2018 (hereinafter: Memorandum of the UK Government on Human Rights, 2018), paragraphs 43–47.

47. Protocol 30 to the TFEU.

48. Art. 1(1), Protocol 30 to the TFEU.

49. Art. 1(2), Protocol 30 to the TFEU.

50. Art. 2, Protocol 30 to the TFEU.

51. EP, Resolution of 12 February 2019, on the implementation of the Charter of Freedoms and Rights of the EU within the EU institutional framework, at http://www.europarl.europa.eu/doceo/document/TA-8-2019-0079_EN.html, 44. A quite unusual remark in an EU document: with Brexit only weeks away (at least so it seemed at the time regret has been expressed), the UK could hardly be affected; it may rather be read, perhaps, as a warning of some sorts for Poland.

52. See the Memorandum of the UK Government on Human Rights (2018), analysing in detail the relation between the EU, ECHR and national sources in Human Rights Law after Brexit, including in the transitional post-Brexit period.

53. Several voices in the UK have been, time and again, been advocating a more or less radical scrapping of the HRA 1998. An example is given by Dearlove's statement cited in the opening of the Introductory Chapter of this book. The Conservative party has repeatedly suggested at all levels that the relation between the UK and the ECHR should be revised, and the HRA substituted by a new Bill of Rights. See the 2014 Conservative party's document. Retrieved from http://news.bbc.co.uk/2/shared/bsp/hi/pdfs/03_10_14_humanrights.pdf. Accessed on April 30, 2019.

HM the Queen stated, in Her speech at the State Opening of Parliament in 2015: 'My government will bring forward proposals for a British Bill of Rights'; followed by Prime Minister Cameron's committing to 'sort out the complete mess of Britain's human rights laws', with a new British Bill of Rights that would 'restore commonsense to our legal system', in an interview to *The Sun* newspaper of June 2015; https://www.bbc.com/news/uk-politics-33134338.

54. *Bunderverfassungsgericht*, cases *Solange I* and *Solange II*; Sirena, 2016, 119.

55. 'Under the Bill, fundamental rights that have been codified in the Charter and which are general principles of EU law will continue to be available and followed for interpretative purposes (see clause 6(3)). However, the Government considers it a natural consequence of the decision to leave the EU – and the UK ceasing to be subject to the requirements that apply to Member state(s) – that the wider role of the general principles 5 should not continue and that UK legal principles and human rights protections should be relied on instead' (Memorandum of the UK Government on Human Rights, 2018, paragraph 47).

56. The Baltic states possibly being a weak link in the EU and NATO security systems, being small, at a short distance from Russian conventional forces, and at high risk of suffering hybrid/non-conventional attacks, in addition to legitimate, non-violent political means from the same neighbouring power (Radin, 2017).

57. The Mitterrand doctrine has *de facto* been scrapped in 2004, with a request for the extradition to Italy of a suspect terrorist endorsed by Prime Minister Raffarin, and the Mitterrand doctrine

then declared deprived of any legal effect by the *Cour de Cassation* (13 October 2004, No. 04-84.470) and the *Conseil d'État* (11–18 March 2005, No. 273714) – with the ECtHR then endorsing the latter decision (decision of 12 December 2006, No. 28796/05).

58. *Associated Provincial Picture Houses Ltd* v. *Wednesbury Corp.* (1948) 1 KB 223.

59. *de Freitas* v. *Permanent Secretary of Ministry of Agriculture, Fisheries, Lands and Housing* [1999] 1 AC69; *Huang* v. *Secretary of State for the Home Department* [2007] UKHL 11, [2007] 2 A.C. 167, [19] citing *R. (Razgar)* v. *Secretary of State for the Home Department* [2004] UKHL 27, [2004] 2 A.C. 368, [20].

60. See Lord Mance in *Kennedy* v. *Charity Commission* [2014] UKSC 20; and in *Pham* v. *Secretary of State for the Home Department* [2015] UKSC 19.

61. Three Justices in the UK Supreme Court expressly supported Prof. Craig's argument in *Pham* v. *Secretary of State for the Home Department* [2015] UKSC 19, [2015] 1 W.L.R. 1591, [60] (Lord Carnwath), [94] (Lord Mance) and [109] (Lord Sumption).

62. 2002/584/JHA: Council Framework Decision of 13 June 2002 on the European arrest warrant and the surrender procedures between Member state(s); OJ L 190/1, 18.7.2002. National implementation laws started being enacted in 2004, making the instrument progressively applicable in all the EU countries.

63. 'Council Decision of 27 November 2014 determining certain consequential and transitional arrangements concerning the cessation of the participation of the United Kingdom of Great Britain and Northern Ireland in certain acts of the Union in the field of police cooperation and judicial cooperation in criminal matters adopted before the entry into force of the Treaty of Lisbon'. OJ L 343/11, 27 November 2014.

64. ACJEU decision issued by the Grand Chamber on 27 May 2019, in joint cases C-508/18 and C 89/19 PPU (ECLI:EU:C:2019:456) on an urgent request of a preliminary ruling endorsed the refusal of execution of an EAW issued by a German prosecutor to be executed in Romania and Lithuania,

based on the argument that German Prosecutors, according to the German Constitution and relevant law, may in some cases be subject to receiving instructions from the relevant *Lander* Ministry of Justice, potentially lacking in some case of independence from the Executive, and not falling thus within the definition of 'judicial authority' within the meaning of Article 6(1) of Framework Decision 2002/584. It is striking how the main European political actor has been cut out of the EAW mechanism – especially considering the rationale provided (prosecutors are subject to some kind of administrative or disciplinary power more or less anywhere). It is still early to assess whether this decision is going to shake the entire EAW system, or whether it is just going to be labelled as an erratic one, to be forgotten as soon as possible.

65. The last published version is in OJ C 335, 6 October 2017.

66. Art. 2(1) of the Framework Decision.

67. Art. 2(2) of the Framework Decision, listing 32 different types of offences, ranging from terrorism to illicit traffic of cultural goods, to arson.

68. Nowhere in the Framework Decision is indicated or may be implied that surrender may be refused based on the relevant person being a national of the requested state. No national reservations have been negotiated by Member state(s) to this principle, except for a specific temporary provision – Art. 33(1) – related to Austria and Austrian citizens permitting such a refusal, at the latest until 31 December 2008.

69. Art. 4 of the Framework Decision.

70. Preamble, Recital (12): 'This Framework Decision respects fundamental rights and observes the principles recognised by Article 6 of the Treaty on European Union and reflected in the Charter of Fundamental Rights of the European Union, in particular Chapter VI thereof. Nothing in this Framework Decision may be interpreted as prohibiting refusal to surrender a person for whom a European arrest warrant has been issued when there are reasons to believe, on the basis of objective elements, that the said arrest warrant has been issued for the purpose of prosecuting or punishing a person on the grounds of his or her sex, race, religion, ethnic origin, nationality,

language, political opinions or sexual orientation, or that that person's position may be prejudiced for any of these reasons.

This Framework Decision does not prevent a Member state(s) from applying its constitutional rules relating to due process, freedom of association, freedom of the press and freedom of expression in other media'.Preamble, Recital (13): 'No person should be removed, expelled or extradited to a State where there is a serious risk that he or she would be subjected to the death penalty, torture or other inhuman or degrading treatment or punishment'.

Article 1(3): 'This Framework Decision shall not have the effect of modifying the obligation to respect fundamental rights and fundamental legal principles as enshrined in Article 6 of the Treaty on European Union'.

71. News given on the same day by the *Financial Times*. Retrieved from https://www.ft.com/content/8facc77a-32af-11e9-bb0c-42459962a812. Accessed on February 19, 2019.

72. House of Commons, Home Affairs Committee, Report of an inquiry on UK–EU security cooperation after Brexit, published on 21 March 2018, item 69. Retrieved from https://publications.parliament.uk/pa/cm201719/cmselect/cmhaff/635/63507.htm.

73. Art. 24 of Council Decision 2009/426/JHA, amending Art. 26 of Council Decision 2002/187/JHA.

74. Art. 23 of Council Decision 2009/426/JHA, inserting Art. 25a in Council Decision 2002/187/JHA.

75. Under Art. 13 of the Convention on Mutual Assistance in Criminal Matters between the Member state(s) of the EU, or under Framework Decision 2002/465/JHA.

76. Said instruments in the Italian law include specific procedural rules, especially on coordination of investigations at national and at a district, supra-local level; specific crime-defining rules; the evidentiary value of former mafia members' confessions, associated with leniency packages and a witness protection program; recourse to armed forces and intelligence services in anti-mafia operations; specific forms of preventive freezing of assets; anti-mafia controls of public procurement processes and financial flows, etc. See the Italian *Codice Antimafia* enacted with *Decreto Legislativo* No. 159 of 6 September

2011, a consolidated set of rules hailing from numerous pieces of legislation spanning well over three decades.

77. Art. 3 of Council Decision 2009/426/JHA, amending Art. 4(1) of Council Decision 2002/187/JHA.

78. Art. 3, Regulation (EU) 2016/794 of the European Parliament and of the Council of 11 May 2016, on EUROPOL, replacing Council Decisions 2009/371/JHA, 2009/934/JHA, 2009/935/JHA, 2009/936/JHA and 2009/968/JHA; OJ L 35 24.5.2016, 53.

79. The list is close but not identical to that provided in Art. 2(2) of the EAW Framework Decision, making EAW applicable without a 'double criminality' requirement when offences are punished with a maximum of at least three years in prison. However, some offences belonging to one list are not in the other, and other ones are substantially coincident but differently labelled.

80. EUROJUST website. Accessed on 10 April 2019.

81. Art. 7, Council Decision 2009/426/JHA, amending Art. 9 of Council Decision 2002/187/JHA, introducing, inter alia, Arts. 9c and 9d.

82. Art. 13 of Council Decision 2009/426/JHA, amending Art. 13 of Council Decision 2002/187/JHA, introducing, inter alia, Art. 13.3.

83. Art. 35 of Council Decision 2009/426/JHA, inserting Art. 39a in Council Decision 2002/187/JHA.

84. Art. 27 of Council Decision 2009/426/JHA, inserting Art. 27A in Council Decision 2002/187/JHA.

85. Regulations (EU) 2018/1727 of 14 November 2018, OJ L 295/138, 21.11.2018.

86. Recital 8, and Art. 50, Regulation (EU) 2018/1727.

87. https://ec.europa.eu/info/law/cross-border-cases/judicial-cooperation/networks-and-bodies-supporting-judicial-cooperation/european-public-prosecutors-office_en#mission

88. Council Regulation 2017/1939 establishing the EPPO, adopted by the JHA Council of 12 October 2017 and entered into force on 20 November 2017.

89. PATRIOT Act, Title III.

90. Treasury Designates Banco Delta Asia as Primary Money Laundering Concern under USA PATRIOT Act. US Treasury press release, 15 September 2005. https://www.treasury.gov/press-center/press-releases/Pages/js2720.aspx.

91. www.britannica.com/biography/Al-Capone

92. See the *Guardia di Finanza* website, www.gdf.gov.it.

93. Art. 86(4) TFEU.

3

THE EU AGENCIES AND OTHER EUROPEAN SECURITY-RELATED INSTITUTIONS AND ARRANGEMENTS

3.1 THE EU FRAMEWORK OF INTERNAL SECURITY

The European Union (EU) has a complex framework of policy and security, which is made by a series of national and international organisations whose jurisdictions often overlap when not clashing with each other. Some of them include non-EU members, whilst others allow them but restrict their prerogatives to a variable extent.

It is not possible for reasons of space to analyse in detail all the existing EU and European agencies and *ad hoc* working groups of which the UK is currently a part of in the areas of security and police; therefore, only a few of them will be covered here. A distinction has to be made between intelligence and law enforcement, with counterterrorism representing an area in the middle, of interest to both, as Table 1 shows.

As it is easy to figure out from Table 1, there is a great degree of overlap amongst them, not only in agencies

Table 1. The EU Security Framework[a]

Intelligence	Terrorism	Law Enforcement
IntCent	the Counter Terrorism Group (CTG)	EUROPOL
the Open Source (OSINT) Division	the EU Situation Room	FRONTEX (border agency)
15 Eyes	European External Action Service (EEAS)	EUROJUST EPPO
Club de Berne		EMCDDA (drugs)
		CEPOL (police college)
		OLAF (anti-fraud office)
		European Multidisciplinary Platform against Crime Threats (EMPACT)

[a]To that list Eu-LISA (management of large-scale IT systems), ENISA (cybersecurity), EASO (asylum), EIGE (gender equality), EMCDDA (drugs), CEPOL (police college) and FRA (fundamental rights) should be added.

belonging to the same field of activity, as it can be expected, but also across different fields – with security and intelligence agencies regularly entering domains that would, on paper, be in the prerogative of law enforcement, and vice versa.

This well-documented phenomenon has created at times confusion and issues. An example is given by the internal struggles between SitCen and EUROPOL when the assessment of intelligence on terrorism is about. SitCen (the precursor of INTCEN) had an input into the Organized Crime Threat Assessment of EUROPOL (Council of the European Union, 2007g), threat analyses of the European border agency FRONTEX (Council of the European Union, 2008i) and EUROJUST (the agency for judicial cooperation in criminal matters, Council of the European Union, 2008o), being on the receiving end of intelligence shared by the Member state(s). However, this also meant that other agencies, such as EUROPOL, received less of the same material.

> *The European Council stated that security and intelligence officials from the member states services should be stationed at EUROPOL to bridge the gap between law enforcement agencies and the security and intelligence services. But only two member states seconded intelligence officials to EUROPOL. EUROPOL concluded that 'it does not expect structured contributions from the side of the intelligence service environment any more' and that this was a clear violation of the political guidelines of the Council. (Buuren, 2013, p. 11)*

One reason for the preference of sharing at SITCEN/INT-CEN level instead of EUROPOL is certainly due to the more restrictive approach observed by the former, in line with the intelligence world's established practices. As a matter of fact, even though

> *data entries can indeed be marked in EUROPOL's databases in order to restrict their further use, this technical system of handling codes does not replace the higher level of confidentiality and interdependence in bilateral intelligence relations. (Bossong, 2018, p. 5)*

Another problem, closely connected to that, has historically been given by the fact that the level of oversight exercised on law-enforcement agencies has always been stricter and more transparent compared to the intelligence sector as a whole, which is by definition the one where successes are secret and only blunders become public. This might prove a hurdle that might undermine data-exchange capabilities of those agencies that are more committed to transparency and stricter administrative rules, such as EUROPOL (Den Boer, Hillebrand, & Nölke, 2008), at a moment when the integration of the internal security sector in the EU brings together agencies hailing from different traditions, in favour of those maintaining a more 'secretive' approach.

The snapshot presented here is not static. The whole sector is in a continuous state of flux – especially so since the attack in Madrid in 2005, which changed a great deal the EU security outlook and accelerated the process of securitisation of terrorist threats in the EU territory, by 'bridging the gap between external and internal security' (Bendiek, 2006, p. 3). The terrorist attacks in Paris in November 2015 boosted the level of intelligence exchanges in Europe, pushing the need for a consolidation of internal security apparatus even further. In this regard, Brexit is only the latest in a long series of shocks to the system, and, like the others, it is going to have a substantial influence on the way the sector works.

Not all agencies and directorates mentioned in Table 1 have the same relevance for the subject covered in this book; this explains the different spaces allotted to them. In any case, all the discussions about intelligence sector at an EU level have to start with the only institution explicitly constituted for the purpose: INTCEN, an entity, somehow surprisingly, not as well-known as it should be.

3.2 THE INTELLIGENCE AGENCY THAT IS NOT: INTCEN

INTCEN has a long history, even though it has changed name a few times since its creation at the moment of the establishment of the European Security and Defence Policy in 1999 at that same moment of the EU Military Staff (EUMS). In its present form, it was created on the ashes of the Joint Situation Centre, SITCEN, established in 2002 as a directorate of the General Secretariat of the Council, directly attached to the office of the High Representative for Foreign Affairs and Security Policy, Dr Javier Solana. At that same moment, intelligence officers from the Member state(s)' services were seconded to EU SITCEN.

SITCEN had no operational role, and it was limited at the onset to sharing assessed intelligence, mainly coming from OSINT (open source), with a view to producing evaluations to support other EU agencies in the elaboration of the EU internal security strategy. However, soon after, it became moving beyond OSINT analysis and sharing nationally sourced classified information. SITCEN

> *began to exchange sensitive intelligence as part of an 'insiders club' made up of intelligence analysts from France, Germany, Italy, the Netherlands, Spain, Sweden and the UK.*[1]

The areas of responsibility of SITCEN continued to expand and, in 2007, it stepped up the collaboration with the EUMS Intelligence Directorate concluding a functional arrangement, called Single Intelligence Analysis Capacity (SIAC), produced for distribution to all Member state(s).[2]

When the Lisbon Treaty entered into force on 1 December 2009, EU SITCEN passed under the direct authority of the High Representative for Foreign Affairs and Security Policy (and Vice President of the EU Commission), becoming part, on 1 January 2011, of the European External Action Service (EEAS). The integration of SITCEN in the wider EEAS framework has not come without a cost, as observed by practitioners as early as 2010.[3] Following further organisational changes in the EEAS in March 2012, SITCEN became INTCEN, still under the direct oversight of EEAS.

On the other hand, the access of the EU Parliament is somehow limited and still under discussion. It is important to highlight that even now, INTCEN is not an autonomous agency, like EUROPOL, being a branch of EEAS instead.[4]

INTCEN is based in Brussels, with a staff of some 100 officers across its divisions recruited from all EU states. His incumbent director is Gerhard Conrad, former Head of the German Intelligence service BDN. INTCEN is currently (2019) structured in two Divisions[5]: INTCEN1, Intelligence, Analysis and Reporting, and INTCEN2, Support/Open Sources Research (OSR). About half of the staff is on secondment from the intelligence and security services of EU Member state(s), whilst about 35 officers, already present in SITCEN, work in the analysis division. Not surprising, considering the fact that INTCEN is part of the EEAS and not an autonomous agency, is the fact that INTCEN does not have its own budget, and all the expenses are covered by the EEAS budget.[6]

One of the main roles of INTCEN today is to support the EU institutions responsible for elaboration of the foreign policy for security and defence, such as the EEAS, by providing the fundamental intelligence components for its formulation. Other institutions too, like the High Commissioners, various EU DG and Member state(s),[7] are frequent users of INTCEN reports. According to some 2014 estimates, the agency produces more than 500 in-between reports and intelligence assessments, which generally cover a short timeframe (between three and six months). They are a kind of analysis that monitors existing areas of tensions and produces evaluation for a rapid response.[8] They are the product of the INTCEN Situation Room, which monitors events on a 24/7 basis.

In terms of philosophical approach, INTCEN, like SITCEN before it, adopts an 'all sources' attitude, exploiting both secret intelligence-driven analysis from Member state(s) and collating information it receives from other EU institutions, such as the EU Satellite Centre. However, it is important to understand that INTCEN maintains some of its predecessor's different characteristics from national intelligence agencies of the kind of MI-6 or the French DGSI, as highlighted by Ilkka Salmi, former head of the Finnish Security Intelligence Service (SUPO) and then director of INTCEN since 2011:

> *INTCEN is not an operational agency. We do not have a collection capability. We do not deal with personal data. We do not carry out clandestine operations. The operational level of intelligence is the member states' responsibility. We only deal with strategic analysis (Salmi, 2014, online).*

The reason for this important difference is not just practical, for example, the small size of INTCEN and the lack of officers to carry out data collection: it is, first and foremost, legal.

Albeit in September 2013 EU commissioner Viviane Reding called (again) for the setting up of an EU-wide fully-fledged intelligence agency just like that of CIA of the United States, the obstacle to something in kind is not budget, but the existing EU law. As a matter of fact, the TEU provides that that national security belongs to the sphere of responsibility of Member state(s) only, not to that of the EU.[9] This provision has historically prevented the creation of a traditionally structured, operationally active intelligence agency at the EU level.

As such, the TEU confines INTCEN (and, previously, SITCEN) to the strategic, advisory role it has today. Any change in this sense would have to come as a modification to the Treaty first:

> *From the legal point of view, it would mean that we would need a treaty change. Then it becomes hugely*

> *political: do we want to do that? What would be the added value, keeping in mind that there's a very intensive cooperation in European intelligence and security services anyway? (Salmi, 2014, online).*

This also might explain one of the main criticisms that have been levelled at INTCEN, and namely, the lack of legal mandate for the institution.

> *INTCEN enjoys no formal legal legitimacy as the Council did not formally adopt a legal act for its establishment as an EU agency. Nor is there a publicly available document with a clearly stated mandate or a similar constituting document. (Statewatch, 2013)*

This bold statement is not entirely correct, despite the fact that a mandate and/or statutory basis akin to those of the US CIA certainly do not exist: INTCEN's legal basis is Art. 4, paragraph 3, sub (a), third indent of the Council Decision (2010/427/EU) of 26 July 2010, which establishes the organisation and functioning of the European External Action Service, and certainly does not violate the provision of Art. 4(2) TEU by providing policy-makers with an instrumental apparatus discharging study, research, analysis and reporting duties.

Whilst INTCEN has its legal basis in EAAS chapters, SITCEN's own legal justification was murkier, since the decision to transfer it to the EU General Secretariat was not made on the basis of a Council Decision but on the initiative of HR Javier Solana (Von Buuren, 2009, quoting Müller-Wille, 2004).

It is important to remember that a great deal of the present EU security framework is due to Solana's view.

> *After 9–11, the High Representative for the Common Foreign and Security Policy, Javier Solana,*

> *put much effort in integrating the fight against terrorism into the EU external relations policy; whereas foreign policy was traditionally relatively absent from EU counterterrorism efforts. (Keohane, 2008, p. 132)*

Moreover, no SITCEN's constituting document has been released. Whatever the case, SITCEN/INTCEN clearly has the political endorsement from the EU and Member state(s) institutions (Ashton, 2013[10]).

Another consequence of the way intelligence is collected there is that INTCEN does not 'own' the information it uses to produce its reports. The information is shared from the single intelligence agencies and services, whose contribution is completely voluntary, and therefore varying a great deal from one year to another and from one state to another. Under this aspect, INTCEN retains the classic approach of the intelligence services around the world, according to which it is the state that sourced and transmitted the intelligence that maintains control over the receiving ends of the information and can decide to restrict it (the so-called 'Third-Party Rule').

As such, INTCEN cannot autonomously decide to declassify[11] these products without getting back to the single Member state(s) originating them; taking into consideration that the different duration of state secrets and the complex regimes the European states have in this respect, it would be particularly difficult to introduce such a policy or practice.

3.3. EUROPOL – THE EU LAW-ENFORCEMENT AGENCY

The importance of EUROPOL, the EU law-enforcement agency in The Hague, the Netherlands, has been growing over the years; a factor mirrored by the growing number of its staff and of liaison officers from third countries. From a small start in 2001, where the unit only employed 323 people, the increase in personnel has been constant over the years, up to 1,203 overall staff in 2017.

The creation of EUROPOL in 1999 predates its status as a formal EU agency, which has only been attained in 2009. On analogous level, ELO (the liaison officers from third parties) have gone up from 73 to 220, as more and more organisations appointed a liaison, amongst which there are INTERPOL, many US federal bodies (e.g. DEA, FBI, FDA, ICE, and IRS) and even US state police entities (NYPD). Another interesting detail is the nationality of the biggest contingents in the office.

According to statistics from the EUROPOL's official website, as of December 2016, and without taking into account the liaison officers, 10 countries in the EU were making up the bulk of the Institution's personnel – namely the Netherlands, Spain, Italy, Romania, Greece, Germany, France, Poland, the UK and Belgium (in order of size of the contingent).

Size of the team apart, the UK has always been a strong supporter, and user, of the EU's crime-fighting agency over the years. Another clear proof of the UK commitment to EUROPOL and its activities is given by the financial contributions made. In 2016, for instance, the UK was the highest contributor to EUROPOL SOC Analysis Projects, and the second highest contributor to the EUROPOL overall, including counter terrorism, after Germany. As of September 2017, the UK was taking part in at least 40 Joint Investigation Teams (JITs) supported by EUROPOL; amongst projects featuring a fundamental British contribution are those related to Firearms, CSEA, Money Laundering, Cyber and Modern Slavery, and Organised Immigration Crime Analysis Project.

Secure Information Exchange Network Application (SIENA) is a particularly important feature of EUROPOL. The SIENA system can be accessed through 95 gateway points across the UK Law-Enforcement community. This consists of 32 NCA access points – which means access directly on the field – for example, in terminals around the United Kingdom, and 63 non-NCA access points. There are currently about 217 officers in the UK Law-Enforcement community who are trained to use the EUROPOL Information System (EIS). EUROPOL's Operational Partners are able to submit EIS data requests through SIENA, whilst the EIS itself is only available to Member state(s).

The importance of EUROPOL extends even further considering the creation of a Public Register, which enhances transparency of the agency's initiatives, and facilitates access from individuals to the EUROPOL documents made available to the public.[12]

The complex and at times difficult cooperation between EUROPOL and the intelligence community has been already highlighted in Section 3.2, discussing INTCEN. This becomes particularly critical in relation to transnational threats like terrorism, and the limited access to intelligence sources can hinder EUROPOL's work. The reform of the body in 2016, which paved the way to further cooperation, aims at reducing these inconveniences.

According to art. 43 (4) of EUROPOL Regulation (EU) 2016/794, the European Data Protection Supervisor has, in principle, access to all data, and this includes nationally sourced classified information.

This is due to the already mentioned fact that law-enforcement agencies are under a stricter discipline than intelligence agencies, when public oversight is about. EUROPOL makes no exception: moreover, a Joint Parliamentary Scrutiny Group (JSG) on EUROPOL was established in 2017.

As it has been observed (Bossong, 2018, p. 8) that 'intelligence services should accept this external control and, more generally, adopt less restrictive interpretations of the so-called Third-Party Rule in the context of exchanges with European oversight bodies'.

The current EUROPOL Director is British former MI-5 Analyst Rob Wainwright, with his tenure ending in mid-2019. The importance of Wainwright's tenure has been fundamental in shaping EUROPOL as it is today, making it 'unrecognisable from the one that went before'; 'most of the systems that make EUROPOL effective are a complete lift and shift from the UK intelligence model' (Parliament.co.uk, 2019, online[13]).

3.4. FRONTEX – THE EU BORDER AND COAST GUARD AGENCY

The Schengen *acquis* eventually departed from the classic model where border security fell within each state's responsibility, to a more complex system in which the EU frontiers' security is in principle granted by the very Union: as a first step towards this end a European Agency for the Management of Operational Cooperation at the External Borders – AKA FRONTEX (a shortened form of French *Frontières Extérieures*) – had been established in 2005. It is tasked with supporting and coordinating EU Member state(s) in their border control efforts.[14]

At its beginning FRONTEX was a small organisation, mostly working in close cooperation with EUROPOL and Schengen governments in a mostly advisory and analytical role, if also featuring its own armed patrols and intervention teams.

With the immigration crisis peak of 2011–2015, however, it became clear that Agency needed a clearer mandate, and a stronger organisation; as well as an EU legal-operational framework for implementing the Union's management system of the Schengen Area external borders, and for repatriation of illegal migrants.[15]

FRONTEX's budget has increased from 6 million euros, in 2005, to 320 million, in 2018.[16] The Agency, which has a staff of some 500, has now some 1,700 officers (2017) deployed at the EU's borders, assisting EU Member state(s)' border security organisations; about 1,500 additional officers may be tasked on short notice to reinforce FRONTEX in case of extraordinary operational needs. During 2018, Jean-Claude Juncker publicly and repeatedly stated the intention of increasing FRONTEX deployed personnel up to 10,000 by 2027 (Angelescu & Trauner, 2018, pp. 1–2).

Border personnel, sea vessels, aircraft and other assets are contributed by EU and Schengen Associated Countries. FRONTEX has the statutory possibility to lease or acquire equipment by itself, or together with a Member state(s) – the latter option permits national matriculation and flag assigned to vessels and aircraft.[17]

The agency was eventually escalated into a fully-fledged EU Border and Coast Guard Agency by Regulation (EU) 2016/1624,[18] maintaining its previous short name of FRONTEX, but having the much wider mission of securing the Schengen area borders in cooperation with Member state(s)' border police and Coast Guard forces – not only related to migration control, thus, but also including crime-fighting, counter terrorism, and intelligence development and sharing[19] – thus becoming a primary asset of the European AFSJ, at least as a vision and in institutional/normative terms, if not (yet) in practical operational ones.

FRONTEX primary duties now also include the enforcement of migration EU rules and repatriation of illegal immigrants, with a right/duty to intervene in international waters and provide SAR activities at sea. Regulation 656/2014 expanded the FRONTEX mandate in the area of maritime operations coordinated by the Agency,[20] with a special view to cases of interception of vessels carrying illegal migrants, providing an obligation to intervene as appropriate with direct police powers, subject to the intervening unit's flag State authorisation, when surveying/intercepting said vessels on the high seas.[21]

Other duties are also on FRONTEX's list of responsibilities, such as networking with EU Member state(s)' and third parties' border security/Coast Guard organisations through its own network of Liaison Officers; producing risk analyses; assessing Member state(s)' border security standards, issuing binding recommendations and assisting Member state(s) in order to improve EU border security.[22]

The agency's earlier mandate and its tiny initial structure confined its previous intelligence role, through the first decade of the twenty-first century, to providing risk analyses to Member state(s) and EU policy organs (the House of Lords Report on FRONTEX, 2007–2008, at 25–27, paragraphs 66–70). The FRONTEX webpage strongly underlines now the intelligence duties discharged by the Agency.[23]

Functions legally entrusted to FRONTEX now include the management of the European Border Surveillance System, EUROSUR, established by Regulation (EU) 1052/2013,[24] providing for

> *a common framework for the exchange of information and for the cooperation between Member States and FRONTEX in order to improve situational awareness and to increase reaction capability at the external borders of the Member States of the Union ('external borders') for the purpose of detecting, preventing and combating illegal immigration and cross-border crime and contributing to ensuring the protection and saving the lives of migrants.*[25]

Art. 2 of Reg. 1052/2013 makes it clear that situational awareness is reached by 'combining new information with existing knowledge' to 'find reasoned grounds for reaction measures' (Art. 2.b), that is, actions 'aimed at countering' (Art. 2.c) 'serious crime with a cross-border dimension committed at, along or in the proximity of, the external borders' (Art. 2.e).

The Agency shall produce

> *situational picture[s] ... to present near-real-time data and information received from different authorities, sensors, platforms and other sources data and information received from different authorities, sensors, platforms and other sources. (Art. 2.d)*

> *The national situational pictures, the European situational picture and the common pre-frontier intelligence picture shall be produced through the collection, evaluation, collation, analysis, interpretation, generation, visualisation and dissemination of information. (Art. 8)*

The subject-matter described in Art. 1 of Reg. 1052/2013, including improving situational awareness and increasing reactivity to combat cross-border crime, is clearly a part of the mission statement of an intelligence organisation. A border and a foreign tactical intelligence one, to be precise, due to its specific responsibilities and outward operational projection, with a view to developing situational pictures functional to immediate operational decisions and action – collecting data from a variety of national, EU and third-party sources, and working in integration with EUROPOL and the Schengen Information System (SIS) to pursue a complex set of objectives well beyond classic border security (Paladini & Castellucci, 2017, p. 3).

The operational/intelligence notions of 'pre-frontier' and 'pre-frontier intelligence picture' are very flexible and interesting: if intrinsically related to a tactical dimension,[26] they may still imply in some cases an operational depths of hundreds or thousands of miles, e.g. at sea or deeply in the African continent or in the Middle East; they may include third countries' territorial waters, seaports or land areas,[27] to be monitored to detect/track/anticipate illegal flows of persons, goods or of the former being treated as the latter, and other serious cross-border crimes-which may include smuggling, terrorism and other illegal activities.

On the other side, the pre-frontier may reasonably need to be operationally coupled with an 'immediate inside', that is, an area inside the EU borders (thus expanding the legal notion of 'at ... or in the proximity of the border' in Art. 2 in Reg. 1052/2013) where FRONTEX may prosecute border-related crimes, without having to stop an action initiated outside to pass the responsibility to national police forces.

Approaches and operational methodologies will necessarily be somehow equivalent to those of military or naval tactical intelligence, including measure and signature intelligence (MASINT) and signals intelligence (SIGINT) activities, with tools of surveillance which may include air/satellite surveillance, sensors, coupled with other forms of data collection, reporting and sharing.[28]

This system is, to some extent, modelled on the Spanish SIVE (*Sistema Integrado de Vigilancia Exterior*) in use to control the Spanish land borders with Morocco, featuring combined physical barriers at the borders and hi-tech with fixed and mobile sensors, radars, cameras and surveillance schemes to provide an early detection of movements towards the Ceuta and Melilla borders, coupled with invasive biometry at the borders for identification and data collection purposes (Benedicto & Brunet, 2018, p. 27).

The Spanish SIVE, in turn, shares the combined physical border infrastructure and hi-tech elements with the US border security system along the frontier with Mexico, as provided since the enactment of the US *Illegal Immigration Reform and Immigrant Responsibility Act* (IIRIRA) of 1996, providing for physical barriers[29] as well as mobile and hi-tech surveillance equipment[30] – with a hundred-of-miles-long wall or, euphemistically, 'secure fence' earnestly being built on the US Southern border until today (Arpaia, 2019).

Despite the absence of walls, or of reinforced physical barriers at most of the EU external borders, the hi-tech part of the Eurosur system has clearly reproduced the main feature of those two models.

Whether FRONTEX operations are conducted by the Agency alone or together with EU Member state(s), NATO, the UN or others, the deployed FRONTEX units would conduct surveillance, collect operational data, and keep it or report it through their chain of command, thus making FRONTEX an immediate collector of raw data and a producer of intelligence.

This would also imply that FRONTEX will now be the owner of its own collected data, and of intelligence produced through its surveillance tools, on its own initiative,[31] thus also being able to classify/declassify information so collected.[32]

The Agency's 'dual-mode' nature, that is, ability to operate both in a 'police' and in a 'military' mode (e.g. when cooperating with the NATO, as in EUNAVFORMED Operation Sophia in the Mediterranean)[33] allows cooperation with a wide variety of EU, national and third-party organisations; thus participating, both as a producer and as an end-user, to the development of a more complex and integrated European intelligence cycle.

On the other hand, it is well possible that FRONTEX participation to the intelligence cycle may be confined to the mostly tactical and very short-term dimensions, the EU environment possibly being less tight in security of classified information than NATO or national traditional intelligence/military environments. More or less, the same developments could take place, *mutatis mutandis*, with EU Battlegroups and other units deployed outside the Union, in relation to the intelligence needed and collected in relation to their activities.

Overall, the expanded responsibilities of the EU institutions do conflict and need somehow to be coordinated with the traditional, different approach of the EU and of EU Member state(s) towards intelligence activities – where the latter maintain data collection activities and control of their intelligence cycle, and the former keeps out of this part of the game.[34]

New scenarios may foster this change of approach in some cases. Very sensitive intelligence may actually be collected by FRONTEX, or also by FRONTEX, for instance, in relation to hybrid threats – normally including a serious cross-border crime dimension (not necessarily illegal immigration) providing the Agency with legal authority to intervene and cooperate with local police, military forces as well as with the EU and NATO ones – for example, in the Baltic area and around the Kaliningrad Russian enclave. Other examples of such cooperation may come from the surveillance of the activities near or at the European terminals of the Chinese 'Silk Road' infrastructural network (e.g. the port of Piraeus, possibly Trieste at some point, or other land terminals within the EU).

It finally needs to be underlined how the UK supported FRONTEX and its collective border security mission since the beginning. However, the UK intention to participate in the adoption of the FRONTEX legal framework and in the organisation and running of the Agency, notified to the Council in 2007, has been turned down first by the European Council, and then by the Court of Justice of the European Union (CJEU)'s Grand Chamber on 18 December 2007,[35] based on the UK not being a Schengen country, and FRONTEX being a Schengen-building measure-not merely a Schengen-related one that could be opted-in to by the UK as a Title IV measure of enhanced cooperation, according to the Treaty of Amsterdam (the House of Lords Report on FRONTEX, 2007–2008, at 23–24, paragraphs 54–60).

To sum up, the UK's intention was clearly that of cherry-picking, participating in the organisation and management of Schengen/FRONTEX without renouncing the control of its national borders, and the CJEU blocked the British attempt. This, however, does not impair the UK's ability to cooperate with FRONTEX as a third country.

3.5. THE SCHENGEN INFORMATION SYSTEM (SIS)

As a necessary implement of the Schengen Area, appropriate platforms for exchanging security-related information have been devised and made operational within the Schengen arrangements and *acquis*.

The SIS has been operational since 1995, pursuant to the Title IV of the Schengen Convention of 1990,[36] to share Schengen countries' national border security authorities records and alerts on persons and objects (e.g. on illegal crossings or attempts at crossing, refusals of entry or stay), including instructions issued by national authorities for individuals associated to an alert.

The development of a second-generation-SIS ('SIS II') has been entrusted to the Commission pursuant to Council Regulation (EC) No. 424/2001 and Council Decision 2001/886/JHA of 6 December 2001, with a view to make SIS available for more general police and judicial cooperation, by allowing competent authorities to create and consult alerts on missing persons and on persons or objects related to criminal offences. SIS II has been established with Regulations (EC) Nos. 1986/2006 and 1987/2006 of the European Parliament and of the Council of 20 December 2006 and with Council Decision 2007/533/JHA of 12 June 2007, and has been operational since 2013, with a centralised database associated with nationally managed ones.

All Schengen Area countries have access to the SIS, including four non-EU states (Switzerland, Norway, Liechtenstein and Iceland) and most EU Member state(s). Bulgaria and Romania have started using the SIS in 2018, whilst still in the process of joining the Schengen Area; Croatia is using the SIS with some restrictions, also being in the process of joining the Area, and a bit further away. Cyprus has a temporary exception from joining the Schengen area and is not using the SIS. The United Kingdom has had full access to the SIS since April 2015, whilst Ireland is still in the process of obtaining it; these two states, however, do not have access to the SIS sub-system of alerts related to refusals of entry or stay in the Schengen Area, not being members of it.[37]

The quantitative aspects of the phenomenon are substantial. As of 31 December 2017, SIS contained approximately 76.5 million records, having been accessed 5.2 billion times and having produced 243,818 hits (i.e. searches leading to a confirmed alert).[38] A total of 1,234,455 UK security alerts have been circulated through SIS II. Some 9,832 UK hits on non-UK alerts and 16,782 non-UK hits on UK alerts have been recorded in 2017. Of the UK hits on non-UK alerts, 97% were terrorists, travelling sex offenders and fugitives, whilst amongst non-UK hits on the UK alerts 94.3% belonged to the same groups.[39]

A comprehensive set of three new Regulations[40] have been enacted by the European Parliament and Council in October–November 2018, to be fully implemented in three years.[41] As a result, Regulation (EU) 2019/1860 deals with immigration control; Regulation (EU) 2019/1861 deals with border control, repealing Reg. 2006/1987; 2019/1862 deals with police cooperation, repealing Reg. 2006/1986.

The devised new SIS features a redefined, wider purpose of the SIS II (Atanassov, 2018), no longer confined to border security but rather wide in providing data exchanges for all AFSJ implementation purposes:

> *The purpose of SIS shall be to ensure a high level of security within the area of freedom, security and justice of the Union including the maintenance of public security and public policy and the safeguarding of security in the territories of the Member States.*[42]

This progressive extension of scope could at some point be matched by the expansion of the European Public Prosecutor's Office (EPPO) competences – considering the more or less parallel initiative of the Commission under the auspices of Jean-Claude Juncker, of September 2018,[43] to entrust the EPPO with the prosecution of cross-border terrorism and other serious transnational crimes.[44] A fully aligned chain of competences integrating EUROJUST, EPPO, EUROPOL and FRONTEX could in due course be established and provided with full access to the Schengen SIS data.

Other purposes of the re-designed SIS include migration control, protection of vulnerable persons, police and judicial cooperation in the seizure of bodies of evidence and other criminal-process-related objects, control of firearms for civilian use.[45] The new SIS will feature new functionalities such as biometric and DNA data management; it should also undergo substantial operational improvements, including better management, better IT performance and the 24/7 basis of functionality of data exchanges,[46] and provide enhanced access to the databases for EUROPOL, EUROJUST and FRONTEX.[47]

The SIS seems heading, to sum up, towards developing soon a state-of-the-art, major security resource. On the other side, a huge amount of data, including sensitive data, will be processed through the SIS IT platforms, subject to stringent rules of data management and data protection, both at EU centralised and at peripheral national level. Would the UK's access to the SIS be lost, after Brexit?

Art. 1 of Reg. 1862/2018 provides that:

> *The purpose of SIS ... [is also] to ensure the application of the provisions of Chapter 4 and Chapter 5 of Title V of Part Three TFEU relating to the movement of persons on their territories, using information communicated through this system.*

Recital 4 of the same Regulation also stresses the pertinence of the SIS rules to Title V.

A non-AFSJ, non-Schengen and non-EU country should thus, in the present legal framework, certainly be denied access to the organisation, development and running of the SIS, unless a special arrangement is designed – for example, agreeing on a case-by-case access to data, or to a special arrangement between the EU and/or all individual Schengen Area countries and the UK – much similarly to what has already happened with the 2007 attempt of the UK to participate in the development of FRONTEX.[48]

A permanent arrangement would imply high costs, let alone possible political oppositions from some EU members, to establish the necessary platform, exchange mechanisms, and implementing rules and protocols. A case-by-case access, on the other side, would certainly produce higher transaction costs and likely operational delays in the daily course of business.

A specific set of provisions should thus be negotiated along the Brexit process to enable the UK to maintain its present form of standing full access to the SIS. However, the validity of such an exception could still be challenged, perhaps – for example, on the grounds of fundamental rights to privacy and data protection, being violated by continent-wide collected data being made automatically available to a third country not being a part of the Schengen framework.

3.6. THE ARCHITECTURE OF THE INFORMATION SYSTEM EXCHANGES – ECRIS

There are a few systems that have been put in place to ensure the smooth exchange of security-related information amongst Member state(s), and one of the most important is the European Criminal Records Information System (ECRIS).

ECRIS has been put in place as early as April 2012, with the Council Framework Decision 2009/315/JHA and Council Decision 2009/316/JHA. As stated on its institutional webpage, the system

> *establishes electronic interconnections between Member States and puts rules into place to ensure that information on convictions as contained in the criminal records system of the Member States can be exchanged through standardised electronic formats, in a uniform and speedy way, and within short legal deadlines.*[49]

The simple idea behind ECRIS is to provide judges and prosecutors from all EU Member state(s) with direct access to comprehensive information on the criminal record of any EU citizen, independently from their nationalities or the place where the offence has been committed. Any criminal conviction of a national of a member State(s) will be shared with the competent authorities of all EU Member state(s), when relevant. Moreover, all crimes committed in any EU country will be coded and reported to the convicted citizen's home country.[50]

Criminal data of physical persons are stored in ECRIS according to a decentralised architecture, which means that there is no central system that owns, stores or elaborates those data from and to criminal records. Every EU country has its national authority storing all criminal records of its own citizens from across Europe, and will provide them to other Member state(s) upon request; both software and databases are operated under the direct responsibility of individual Member state(s). Internal laws and procedures on data-handling and data protection, thus, apply in each Member state(s) – which could potentially represent an issue given the disparities in security standards, as well as in rules on transparency and access to data, amongst different Member state(s).[51]

Mechanisms such as ECRIS platform have been used with success over the years; many reports indicate how valuable they are to Member state(s). This is one of the areas, amongst many, that are going to be severely affected by Brexit: for reasons that that have already been highlighted in the introduction, it is likely that Brexit's impact on law enforcement and police work will be harder than on intelligence sharing at a more traditional level.

An estimate has already been made, at least from the UK's side, on the 'dividends' (to use a word dear to Brexiteers) of the cooperation with the EU in terms of crime prevention and information sharing in security. In a written evidence regarding 'Brexit and EU policing and security cooperation' due to David Armond's letter of 15 December 2016, the National Crime Agency provided updated statistics on the UK use of EU-related databases and legal frameworks.

The results speak by themselves: ECRIS makes the whole procedure of information checking straightforward and remarkably fast. At the moment, criminal record checks amongst EU Member state(s) take six days on average, whilst the time needed with third countries is far lengthier: about 66 days on average, often longer than that.[52]

ECRIS has also been extensively used, for example, in the case of requests made for employment purposes in relation to children, in order to screen for recorded offenders. Another of ECRIS use is in relation with ACRO[53] (the UK Criminal Records Office), the national agency that manages the UK Central Authority for the Exchange of Criminal Records

(UKCA-ECR). According to official data, in 2016 ACRO exchanged 173,251 requests and notifications with the EU, the majority of them channelled by ECRIS, registering a 30% increase in requests from the EU for the past three years.

Recourse to European Arrest Warrants – whose legal details have been discussed in Chapter 1 – has become quite common in the EU; 1,735 individuals have been arrested in the UK based on an EAW between 2016 and 2017. This takes the total number of arrests in the UK with an EAW to some 12,000 since April 2009.

3.7. THE EUROPEAN CYBERSECURITY AGENCY (ENISA)

Based in Athens and Heraklion, this EU cybersecurity agency has been established in 2004, with a fixed-term duration of five years. Its mandate has been subsequently renewed and expanded in 2007, 2011 and 2013; and finally in 2019[54] when, based on a wider vision, ENISA became a standing EU body without any fixed-term mandate, with an enhanced role and increased budget.[55] This occurred following a 2016 Directive establishing a common EU framework of requirements, obligations and actions in the areas of cybersecurity and cybercrime.[56]

ENISA has the mission of supporting the EU, EU Member state(s), and private market stakeholders (e.g. digital market actors) in developing cybersecurity within the framework of EU policy and instruments, and preventing and dealing with cyber incidents with a cross-border dimension. The Agency's mission is accomplished, inter alia, through research, analyses of risks, threats, vulnerabilities, incidents – activities implying a substantial cyberintelligence dimension; and by capacity-building, education and awareness-rising actions.[57]

The agency shall cooperate with other EU agencies, Member state(s), as well as private stakeholders (a number of which sit in the Agency's Advisory Group).[58] ENISA's duties include issuing recommendations and advice, and staging cybersecurity excersises in cooperation not only with Member state(s) but also with OECD, OSCE and NATO.[59]

One of the notable features of the 2019 EU Cybersecurity Act (Reg. 2019/881) is the creation of a EU area of direct and supranational responsibility in a specific matter of security, if possibly still considered by some as an indirect, non-core dimension of security concerns: ENISA will have responsibility for the security certification and the related standard-setting for ICT products, processes and services, with a view to protecting the security of the digital single market; and for the certification of the related national certifying authorities of Member state(s).[60] The security certification is a non-mandatory system thus far, which may still at some time or for some specific areas or certification schemes become mandatory.[61]

National cybersecurity authorities shall be established by Member state(s), replicating to a significant extent ENISA's functions and complementing them nationally, to produce an integrated EU-wide network devised and empowered by the EU Cybersecurity Act.[62]

The original rule laid in Reg. 460/2004 first establishing ENISA made it open to the participation, through operational agreements, of non-EU countries required having agreed to adopt the EU legislation in the areas covered by those Regulations – a reference to European Economic Area (EEA) countries such as Norway, Iceland, Lichtenstein; the former two also being NATO-members.[63]

The original need to adopt the EU law for third countries to be admitted to the ENISA's activities (Art. 24 Reg. 2004/460), which had consistently been maintained in all subesequent instruments renovating the agency's mandate until 2015, has been dropped after the Brexit referendum: Art. 42.1 of Reg. 2019/881 now permits cooperation between ENISA and third parties, such as non-EU countries and international organisations; Art. 42.2 provides that the agency shall be open to third countries having concluded agreements with the EU to that effect.

Brexit, thus, will of course exclude the UK from any role in developing ENISA's mandate, as well as in the agency's governance; and the devised EU cybersecurity certification system will not be relevant for the UK. Cooperation, however, will still be possible according to Art. 42 of the EU Cybersecurity Act, within the framework of a bilateral agreement clarifying objectives, forms and allocation of costs of the relevant cooperation. The UK as agreeing third party should also, most likely, more or less explicitly agree to be bound by the agency's working rules based on the EU-law, as far as they are relevant for the specific activities concerned – including, e.g., EU rules on protection of personal data,[64] and of sensitive non-classified and EU-classified information.[65]

3.8. OTHER EUROPEAN INSTITUTIONS AND ARRANGEMENTS DEALING WITH INTELLIGENCE AND INTERNAL SECURITY

A final note on the other agencies, listed in Fig. 3.1. As mentioned before, there are many other formal and informal institutions and mechanisms set up at an EU level, in addition to those analysed in this Chapter and that deal in a direct or indirect way with intelligence, law enforcement and security as a whole. A detailed analysis of all of them is outside the scope of this book, mostly focussed on the overall security architecture rather than on the various related agencies.[66]

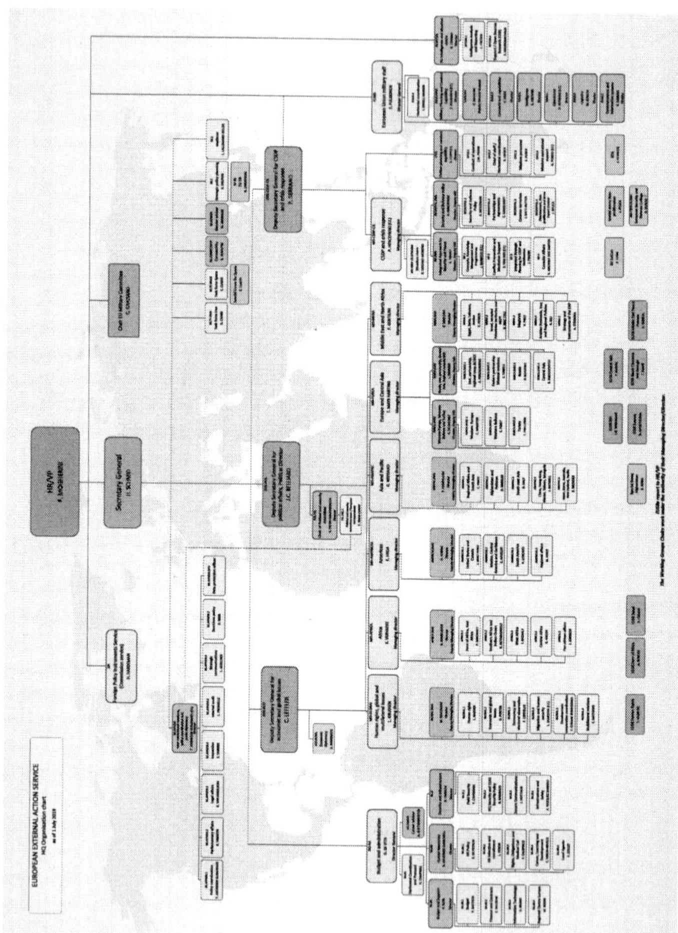

Fig. 3.1. European External Action Service (EEAS) – Organisation Chart.

Here, it is worth mentioning the ones, such as the European Multidisciplinary Platform against Crime Threats (EMPACT), which are directly connected with EUROPOL and bound to have a growing importance in the ongoing four years (2018–2021) EU Policy Cycle. As explained on the EUROPOL page, a four-year policy cycle was set up in 2010 with the Council Conclusions on the creation and implementation of a EU policy cycle for organised and serious international crime (doc. 15358/10), to set up to ensure continuity in the fight against international and organised crime.[67]

EMPACT, the third of four steps in the implementation of the Policy Cycle,[68] is organised around a series of priority actions and projects that bring together and coordinate ongoing activity by Member state(s) and their organisations against a set of threats, codified in 'EMPACT priorities' – currently in the number of 13.

The UK participates in all of them, exercising the role of 'Driver' (project leader) in two (Trafficking in Human Beings [THB] and Excise Fraud,) and as a 'Co-Driver' in other four (MTIC – Missing Trader Intra-Community – Fraud, Drugs, Criminal Finances – Money Laundering/Asset Recovery and Firearms). A total of 150 operations have been carried out amongst the various EMPACT priorities in 2018, with the UK leading 25 of them (about 17%).

Not all of institutions listed in Fig. 3.1 are, however, EU agencies or directorates. There are other groups and institutions dealing at some title with European internal security that, whilst enjoying cooperation with the EU, are not technically EU structures themselves, and therefore not subjected to EU rules and oversight.

A well-known one is the Counter-Terrorist Group (CTG),[69] which includes all the EU Member state(s), Norway and Switzerland. CTG is actually one of the oldest joint European initiatives addressing terrorism, having been created just after 9/11.

One of its features is the institutional coverage of a variety of technical operations in a cooperative setting, both at a multinational and a bilateral level. It provides a communications network amongst intelligence and security services for sharing sensitive information. Because of this, CTG is a very valuable resource, including for the UK:

> *they look at best practices together and since this is spooks with spooks, they get on pretty well and do quite a bit of decent stuff. They have kept the EU reasonably away from that, which is legitimate.*[70]

Another is the Club de Berne, which is somehow wider in scope than the CTG, from which, however the CTG has come from. The Club de Berne is an informal gathering of the heads of the security and intelligence services of EU states, Norway and Switzerland, and it goes back as early as the 1970s.

> *It is the principal point of contact of the European heads of national security services and has established working groups on terrorism and organized crime. The Club de Berne does not base its activities on a formal charter and operates outside of the institutions of the EU.*[71]

Whilst originally intended for dealing with terrorism, after the creation of CTG the Club 'outsourced' the responsibility over the area to this newer structure, concentrating instead on counterintelligence as a whole.

In parallel to what has already been observed for other security institutions, CTG has changed a great deal since its creation, as well. At the very beginning, the CTG worked on a case-by-case approach, which only occasionally involved consultations at the EU level. Paris attacks in 2015 produced the result of strengthening the institute itself and the related cooperation.

> *In 2016, the CTG opened permanent headquarters in The Hague. There, liaison officers of the participating intelligence services can access their respective national information systems as well as edit a common database. This should provide for a much more comprehensive picture of terrorist networks in Europe.*[72]

Since these institutions do not formally belong to the EU's security framework, they are likely to keep working unaffected by the kind of agreements (or lack of) a post-Brexit Europe is going to negotiate.

NOTES

1. Nomikos (2015, online).
2. EU INTCEN Factsheet (2018).
3. 'One positive thing about SitCen was that it brought together a range of information stakeholders, particularly military and foreign intelligence services and security services […] It was able to produce all sorts of assessments covering the whole picture, so if you were looking at Al-Qaida you did not stop by looking at it just within your own borders or outside your borders, it was looked at as a whole. The worrying thing as Lisbon approached was in how to make sure that that was not damaged, because everyone realised that with the creation of the EEAS, although it was intended […] to increase the coherence of our external action, to a certain extent there is a disassociation of that external action from some other spheres of activity.

   Wherever you put the SitCen – if you put the SitCen in the EEAS, you have to work back to your customers dealing with the internal; or, you split the SitCen, but that was not a very good idea; or, you leave the SitCen in some other structure where one of its main customers would of course be the External Action Service – there was no neat answer. A decision was taken, probably because the bulk of its work is in the external area, to put it in the EEAS. [...] They made it clear that it was to continue to provide its services to the other bodies of the Council, to the Commission and to the President of the European Council [...] The mechanical steps have been taken to preserve this capacity to work for the other structures, but of course, information-sharing is not just about mechanics. It is about confidence and understanding, and it is a bit early to see whether its organisational placement has any effect on that' (Shapcott, 2010, online).

4. In the rest of the book, INTCEN has been defined as the 'agency' for convenience, but it is important to remember this detail, as explained later in the section when talking about its legal basis. The full organisation chart of EEAS is available at https://eeas.europa.eu/sites/eeas/files/2019-01-03_-_eeas_2.0_orgchart_update.pdf, included also here.

5. Formerly (2015), the institution included four divisions: Analysis, Open Source (OSINT) Division, the EU Situation Room and the Consular Crisis Management Division: it has since then been restructured, the Situation Room currently being under the different CSDP and Crisis Response Department (https://eeas.europa.eu/topics/crisis-response/412/crisis-management-and-response_en).

6. EU INTCEN Factsheet (2018).

7. It is important to note that, whilst INTCEN 'expects all its members to be EU citizens', it shares its reports with all the Member state(s), had they contributed or not to the data collection.

8. Similarly to what happen at the CIA, there are intelligence reports produced and circulated every week, and a daily intelligence highlight aimed at EEAS's senior management.

9. TEU, Art. 4(2).

10. Lady Catherine Ashton was at that time the head of the EEAS and also the High Representative of the Union for Foreign Affairs and Security Policy.

11. In line with other intelligence agencies, INTCEN uses a series of labels for its reports. 'LIMITED' is the lowest – and it means that the report contains no classified information. The others, which progressively restrict access, are called 'EU RESTRICTED', 'EU CONFIDENTIAL', 'EU SECRET' and 'EU TOP SECRET'. According to internal sources, half of INTCENT reports are 'EU

Restricted', whilst the 'TOP SECRET' is, not surprisingly, the rarest classification label.

12. This measure is part of the implementation of the principle of transparency and the rights for individuals to access documents of EU bodies stated in Article 15 of the TFEU and Article 42 of the Charter of Fundamental Rights of the EU. Regulation (EC) No. 1049/2001.

13. Quoting David Armond, then Deputy Director General of the UK National Crime Agency (NCA).

14. As established by Council Regulation (EC) 2007/2004 of 26 October 2004, OJ L 49, 25 November 2004. Additional competences have been given to the Agency with subsequent Regulations of the European Parliament and the Council Regulations Nos. 863/2007 and 1168/2011, until Regulation 2007/2004 was ultimately repealed with the 2016 Council Regulation establishing the new FRONTEX Agency.

15. As per Articles 77 and 79 TFEU, Regulation (EU) 2016/399 on the rules governing the movement of persons across borders (Schengen Borders Code), and Directive 2008/115/EC of the European Parliament and of the Council of 16 December 2008, on common standards and procedures for returning illegal migrants.

16. https://frontex.europa.eu/faq/key-facts/

17. https://frontex.europa.eu/faq/key-facts/

18. Regulation (EU) 2016/1624 of 14 September 2016 on the European Border and Coast Guard, OJ L 251, 16 September 2016, 1, which also integrated and referred to the previous EUROSUR Regulations 1052/2013 and 656/2014.

19. See the Foreword and the Statement of Mission of FRONTEX in its webpage, at Frontex.europa.eu.

20. Regulation (EU) 656/2014 of 15 May 2014, establishing rules for the surveillance of the external sea borders in the context of operational cooperation coordinated by the European Agency for the Management of Operational Cooperation at the External Borders of the Member state(s) of the European Union, OJ L 189/93, 27 June 2014.

21. Reg. 656/2014, Art. 8.

22. Foreword, FRONTEX webpage, Frontex.europa.eu.

23. Statement of Mission, FRONTEX webpage.

24. Regulation (EU) 1052/2013 of 22 October 2013, establishing the European Border Surveillance System (Eurosur), OJ L 295/11, 6 November 2013.

25. Recital I and Art. 1 of Reg. 1052/2013.

26. Reg. 1052/2013, (Art. 2.g): 'pre-frontier area' means the geographical area beyond the external borders'.

27. Arts. 11 and 12, Reg. 1052/2013.

28. Art. 12.3, Reg. 1052/2013.

29. IIRIRA, Section 102.

30. IIRIRA, Section 103.

31. Reg. 1052/2013, Art. 12.5.

32. See discussion *supra*, Section 2.2.

33. See the related webpage on the Italian ministry of Defence web portal, at https://www.difesa.it/OperazioniMilitari/op_intern_corso/eunavfor_med/Pagine/default.aspx.

34. See discussion *supra*, Section 2.2.

35. CJEU, Grand Chamber, *United Kingdom* v. *Council*, C-77/05, Judgment delivered on 18 December 2007, ECLI:EU:C:2007:803; and Opinion of Advocate General Trestenjak of 10 July 2007, ECLI:EU:C:2007:419.

36. See the page devoted to the SIS on the European Commission's webpage https://ec.europa.eu/home-affairs/what-we-do/policies/borders-and-visas/schengen-information-system_en.

37. See the SIS webpage on the European Commission's portal.

38. SIS webpage.

39. Home office, cited.

40. Regulations (EU) Nos. 2019/1860, 2019/1861, 2019/1862 of 28 November 2018.

41. Legislative Resolution of the EP of 24 October 2018, and Council Decision of 19 November 2019.

42. Art. 1, Reg. 1862/2018.

43. Supra, Chapter 2, Section 2.7

44. An expansion possible according to Art. 86(4) TFEU.

45. Art. 47, Reg. 1862/2018.

46. All mentioned topics are dealt with in Reg. 1862/2018.

47. Arts. 48, 49 and 50, Reg. 1862/2018.

48. See discussion above, end of Section 3.4, and the related case *United Kingdom* v. *Council*, CJEU, Grand Chamber, C-77/05, Judgment delivered on 18 December 2007, ECLI:EU:C:2007:803; and Opinion of Advocate General Trestenjak of 10 July 2007, ECLI:EU:C:2007:419.

49. ECRIS (2019).

50. This is the case even if the crime a person is convicted for in the other country is not a crime in the person's home country, the record will be nonetheless sent over. However, only criminal cases are covered by ECRIS. No information will be shared if a person has not been convicted in a criminal court, or if the case has not reached a criminal court, whatever the reason.

51. In the UK, for instance, citizens are allowed to put in a request through ECRIS to access information on their own criminal record.

52. NPCC (2019).

53. ACRO was founded in 2006, with the aim of establishing 'an operationally focussed unit to organise the management of criminal records information and improve the links between criminal records and biometric information', (ACRO, 2019, online), and it has grown substantially since then, with more than 300 officers at the moment. ACRO also notifies Member state(s) of the convictions of citizens from the EU Member state(s) when living in the UK (35,509 in 2016 only).

54. Regulation (EU) 2019/881, the new EU Cybersecurty Act, repeals the previous Reg. (EU) 2013/526, which in turn had repealed the original Reg (EC) 2004/460 establishing ENISA.

55. Reg. 2019/881, Recitals (19) and (64).

56. Directive (EU) 2016/679 of 6 July 2016, OJ L 194, 19.7.2016, p.1

57. see "About" on the ENISA webpage; https://www.enisa.europa.eu/about-enisa

58. Reg. 2019/881, Art. 21.

59. Reg. 2019/881, Recitals (43) and (44). The first EU-wide cybersecurity exercise, Blue Olex, has taken place in early July 2019,

about one week the entry into force of the new Cybersecurity Act, witth cooperation of Member state(s)' security and intelligence agencies and ENISA. Large-scale EU cybersecurity exercises are expected to take place regularly, on a biennial basis (Reg. 2019/881, Art. 7.5).

60. Reg. 2019/881, Recitals from (65) to (107), and provisions in Title III (Arts. 46-62).

61. Reg. 2019/881, Recital (92).

62. Reg. 2019/881, Art. 58.

63. Reg. 2004/460, Art. 24.1.

64. Art. 41 Reg. 2019/881, making a direct reference to Regulation (EU) 2018/1725 on Protection of personal data.

65. Art. 43 Reg. 2019/881, making a direct reference to Regulations (EU, Euratom) 2015/443 and 2015/444, on the protection of sensitive unclassified data and EU classified information, respectively

66. Additional information about them can be retrieved on the EU portal.

67. 'On 27 March 2017, the Council decided to continue the EU Policy Cycle for organised and serious international crime for the period 2018–2021. This multi-annual Policy Cycle aims to tackle the most important threats posed by organised and serious international crime to the EU in a coherent and methodological manner through improving and strengthening co-operation between the relevant services of the Member state(s), EU institutions and EU agencies as well as third countries and organisations, including the private sector where relevant' (EUROPOL, 2019, online).

68. For the four steps of the policy cycle and a more precise definition of EMPACT scopes, see: https://www.europol.europa.eu/empact.

69. The CTG should not be confused with the ECTC, The European Counter Terrorism Centre (ECTC), which has been created within the EUROPOL in 2016, in the aftermath of Paris attack, together with a reform of the EUROPOL to foster additional integration amongst Member state(s).

70. Shapcott (2010, online).

71. Walsh (2006, p. 631).

72. Bollard (2018, p. 11).

4

WHAT LIES AHEAD? A POST-BREXIT SCENARIO ANALYSIS

4.1 CHANGING GEOPOLITICAL AND SECURITY SCENARIOS

It seems likely that post-Brexit UK will try and revise its foreign policy and grand strategy in favour of its historical Atlantic axis with the United States; however, the growing nationalist–protectionist sentiment developing there may require the UK to maintain and even improve cooperative ties with the EU (Hayes, 2019; Hill, 2019). It is also possible that the UK will try to improve its ties with some of the Anglosphere and Commonwealth countries, with a view of regaining some of its political critical mass and lost centrality on the global scene (Gamble, 2019; Hill, 2019, pp. 105–109; Pierce, 2019) – including some leverage for pursuing its national interest through votes in multilateral fora (e.g., to impose sanctions on a third country, no longer being able to prime or participate in a EU sanctioning process).

Its nuclear deterrence and United Nation Security Council (UNSC) permanent membership, the preferential relation with the United States and the participation in the Five

Eyes arrangement will help Britain in maintaining a military power status, probably more than its NATO membership; and certainly more than any European Union (EU) military arrangement, towards which the UK has always displayed little enthusiasm during its EU-membership years – certainly preferring to support a closer security cooperation between the EU and the NATO, rather than a growing autonomous military role of the former (Hayes, 2019, p. 17; Hill, 2019, pp. 87–92).

A significant military power role for the UK may come from cooperation with France, pursuing the St Malo summit of 1998 and the Lancaster House treaty of 2010, with which the two medium-large-size powers have tried to take the lead in European – not just EU – military affairs.

The relation between the UK and Germany may be more difficult to assess in the long term, due to their opposing historical geopolitical roles and traditions, well known in classic geopolitical theories (Mackinder, 1904; Spykeman, 1944), as well as to more recent, present and probably also future leaning of said countries in their strategic expansion, respectively, towards the Atlantic and in the relation to the United States, on one side; and towards the Eurasian continent, including a (Germanised) EU, Russia and China, on the other.

Economic changes brought about by Brexit may affect the security-providing capacity of the country: industrial capacity will still make the UK a major provider of military and security equipment, despite the increase in costs and difficulties in cooperative ventures involving EU-based producers: however, specific arrangements should be found, in pursuing a win–win abatement of trade- and customs-related costs for strategic and/or marketable security-related productions. Brexit-related economic changes may also affect the UK security capacity in a different way: a loss of value of the Pound Sterling may, at least to some extent, reduce the financial capacity of the UK government and the country in its entirety; as a consequence, budget constraints may affect – as they usually do – defence and security research, development and procurement expenditure in a higher-than-proportional fashion, due to the higher priority normally given in such situations to basic general needs and social expenditure (Ferreira Nunes, 2017).

Finally, Brexit would certainly have some short- and medium-term impact on established mechanisms providing security, due to the changes in the legal and institutional frameworks. Probably, a stronger impact will be felt on the law-enforcement side, which is more affected by the institutional change; and a lesser impact on the areas traditionally more related to the sovereign activities of individual Member state(s), like defence and intelligence. An in-between-size impact is likely to be felt, both qualitatively and quantitatively, in relation to hybrid areas like counterterrorism.

It could be tempting to establish a relation between the 2016 Brexit referendum and all the subsequent important reforms of EUROJUST, the European Public Prosecutor's Office (EPPO), EUROPOL, FRONTEX, Schengen, ENISA, and European data management – all having been reviewed, strengthened, expanded, and made more consistent between 2016 and 2019.[1] It is also remarkable how the European Defence debate too has been revived after 2016.[2] A question needs perhaps to be asked, about Brexit having or not been a primer or accelerator in the development of a more secure EU (at least in normative and institutional terms, thus far). Should the answer be a positive one, we would have been witnessing a win–win process, producing a more secure insular UK (with Ireland?) and a more secure EU.

4.2. BREXIT: 'DE-MYTHOLOGISING' THE CURRENT DEAL/NO-DEAL DEBATE TO FOCUS ON LONG TERM, FRAMEWORK SOLUTIONS

Brexit may certainly prove a lose-lose development, at least in the area of security and law enforcement, if cooperation in those fields if impaired or discontinued. Cooperative schemes are needed, ideally, before the deadline; or later, more realistically, but with a transition period during negotiations of new cooperation arrangements in which cooperation should proceed, to avoid the disruption possibly produced by a cliff-edge-style, immediate discontinuing of operations.

Excluding for a moment a 'Bremain' option – unlikely, but not entirely to be ruled out – possible post-Brexit developments would thus include a 'deal' and a 'no-deal' scenario.

A 'deal' providing for a transition period would just permit addressing the impact of Brexit on actual public and private life of either side more appropriately, adjusting policies and rules accordingly. A 'no deal' would lead to a probably complicated, possibly chaotic situation – some would say a nightmare, Halloween scenario – at midnight, Brussels time (11 p.m. in London), 31 October 2019.

Before the end of the two-year period provided for in Art. 50 TEU for the withdrawal notice issued by the UK on 29 March 2017 to have effect, the deadline has been extended twice (thus far): first from 29 March to 12 April 2019; then again to 'no later than' 11 p.m., London time, 31 October 2019 (it could also be before that date). The postponements have been due to the UK's internal difficulties in determining how to implement the 2016 Referendum result.

The 'deal' proposed by Prime Minister May has repeatedly been rejected by the Parliament. British politics has not been able, since then, to decide whether to try again to negotiate an orderly transition, through legislative and administrative arrangements, or to move towards a no-deal, 'hard' Brexit.

However, it is important to notice that the 'deal' discourse proposed by Prime Minister May was centred on determining transition periods and mechanisms for the phasing out of different areas of the EU law.[3] The 'deal' proposed in the 2017 draft agreement was, in fact, an agreement to conclude subsequent agreements in various areas, within one-and-a-half to two-and-a-half years – maintaining meanwhile the EU laws and arrangements applicable to and in the UK – also determining distributions of the associated costs between the parties.

There is no guarantee, thus, that such a 'deal' would really represent a final solution to Brexit-related problems; two full years after the Brexit referendum have been spent, indeed, negotiating a deal to prolong the EU law in the UK for two more years. It could well be, should this kind of 'deal' solution ultimately be achieved, that one or more agreed transition periods eventually come to their end without any longer-term arrangement or set of arrangements made in some critical area; returning, thus, to a no-deal-Brexit situation, only delayed.

Still, the development of appropriate forms of cooperation, including a legal framework, institutional links and operational practices between the UK and the EU will need to be attempted, preferably during a transition period, to avoid legal loopholes producing security gaps and issues, and to avoid discontinuing parts of the existing cooperation.

In any case, the UK shall take unilateral steps in the domestic domain to govern the transition of the UK legal system out of the EU one, avoiding leaving legal gaps and shockwaves, and preserving the system's functionality as well as consolidated rights in the law of the land. The EU (Withdrawal) Bill of 2017 is clear with respect to this, as it is the UK Government White Paper on related legislative needs.[4]

UK domestic law and its interoperability with the EU and EU Member state(s) law(s) will remain important for security-related matters: whilst it is safe to assume that most of the EU law will be 'domesticised' on Brexit Day Zero, and that the UK's European Convention on Human Rights membership will be maintained, it is also reasonable to imagine a divergence in subsequent domestic legal developments, possibly affecting the outcomes of subsequent cooperation.

In conclusion, trying to simplify the security-related issues produced by Brexit, it could be said that for both the UK and the EU there is a urgent need to address three main issues (the Irish border, fundamental rights and judicial cooperation, and police cooperation), and consider two-plus-one main framework solutions (a 'Norwegian' solution and a 'Swiss' solution; plus a total or partial permanence of the UK in the customs union and single market, or the conclusion of new trade agreements, to simplify the Irish border issue as well).

Extra details, variations, combinations of elements may be included of course in this very simple description – basically, just a memory prop – of 'three issues, and two-plus-one framework solutions', developed in Sections 4.3–4.6.

4.3. CRITICAL POINTS: EUROPOL

It is impossible to foresee which kind of regulatory framework will take the place of the existing one. However, it is certain that the already mentioned possible developments in the UK's law on fundamental rights are going to affect the UK access to pan-European law enforcement, judicial cooperation and their smooth functionality.

The first and more important case regards EUROPOL.

> *EUROPOL is the jewel in the crown of EU law enforcement cooperation. Under the able and*

> *effective leadership of its current Director, Rob Wainwright, it has become an invaluable tool in the fight against international terrorism, serious organised crime and cybercrime. In an increasingly interconnected world, with many serious crimes crossing borders or taking place online, it has never been more vital for UK law enforcement agencies to work in partnership with their counterparts across Europe. From the evidence received, it is clear to us that there can be no substitute for UK access to EUROPOL's capabilities and services, and that maintaining this should be a key priority in the Brexit negotiations. (Parliament.uk, online, 2018)*

A possibility that applies to more than one scenario is that the UK will leave EUROPOL (the membership of which is only open to the EU Member state(s)). In both cases, it is easy to imagine that the UK will maintain a number of liaison officers (ELOs) in EUROPOL, and, as the agency provides support even to non-EU Member state(s), that it will continue to take part in its activities.

There are two ways this can happen: there are two distinct forms of partnerships with third countries, as stated on the EUROPOL website: one is called 'strategic agreement', and covers the exchange of general intelligence and strategic and technical information; and the second is, more extensive and comprehensive than the previous one, 'operational agreement', of the kind EUROPOL has with sovereign states such as the US and Switzerland, and agencies such as Interpol. There are about 20 operational partners as now, but they do not contribute case officers or sit on the EUROPOL Management Board. Moreover, whilst they cannot lead projects, they can still join them, and, considering the many common interests between the UK and the EU Member state(s) when fighting international crime and terrorist threats, it is to be expected the UK will.

Still, leaving the agency would have an immediate and profound impact, and even most worrying is the uncertainty of the kind of agreement the UK is going to put in place after Brexit.

It is important to remember that the abovementioned existing operational agreements came into effect before the agency obtained its current status and adopted the so-called EUROPOL Regulation. As a result, it will have to take a road never before taken. According to the new legal framework, two routes are available for achieving an operational agreement, one as a treaty including justice and home affairs and another where the EU Commission makes 'a data adequacy decision' (Parliament.uk, online). However, it remains always possible – and this is the clear intention of the UK – to achieve a bespoke agreement with EUROPOL that will preserve at the maximum possible the current security capabilities. There is a precedent in this sense: Denmark. Whilst remaining a current EU member, Denmark has renegotiated its status with EUROPOL, after a referendum in December 2015, with which it has opted out of EU Area of Freedom, Security, and Justice (AFSJ),[5] obtaining a hybrid agreement, between a full EU member's AFSJ participation and a merely operational agreement.

It remains to be seen if such a type of bespoke, tailor-made deal is available to the UK, and a few observers have declared it unlikely. In any case, a bespoke deal granting higher access than the one granted by an operational agreement would require at the very least the recognition of the Court of Justice of the European Union (CJEU)'s jurisdiction in the territory (Dashwood, 2017), which is something the UK has no intention of giving. Whatever the form of the relationship between the UK and EUROPOL is going to take, in immediately practical terms, a few operational arrangements will have to change, starting from project management.

As of February 2019, the UK is still the leading part in four of the 13 main project units, with a status of relevance in a number of others.

> *The NCA's recent evidence stated that the UK currently has 'project driver' status in two priorities and co-driver status in a further four, and is leading 25 of the 150 operational actions planned for 2018. (Parliament.uk, online, 2018)*

This is going to change and the UK will only be able to join existing projects but not strategically inform, let alone lead them. Moreover, the UK will lose the enhanced level of access to EUROPOL's main database, the EUROPOL Information System, which, as mentioned above, is only open to the Member state(s). In future, as a third country, the UK will have to use SIENA to channel the information and the request and it will have to wait for one of the head units to get back to them, which, of course, will delay the answers. Which kind of input at strategic level and the level of access allowed in participating and sharing initiatives remains to be seen.

Another area where the impact of leaving the EU in a solution that does not include a full access to the Common Market (such as Norway, for instance) and the law-enforcement agencies is the use of the European Criminal Records Information System (ECRIS), which has been shown to be critical. Whilst the database works well with regard to the EU citizens, this is not the case at the moment with non-EU citizens, because, for the way the system is designed, when a criminal court in a Member state(s) convicts a non-EU citizen, that information is stored only locally and not shared with the others. No central reference point exists for a non-EU national's criminal record, and Member state(s) cannot know of any previous criminal records.

> *A complete overview of an individual's convictions can only be obtained by sending a 'blanket' request for information to all Member States. Because this causes significant administrative burdens for the authorities of the Member States, this possibility is rarely used at the moment. (Europe-Nu, 2019, online)*

This is going to create issues at the moment the UK itself becomes a third-country, thus losing its access to the system. As far as an agreement is not reached, the post-Brexit UK-EU cooperation in this field would suffer a major blow – more or less setting the clock back to the times of the Council of Europe Convention on Mutual Assistance in Criminal Matters of 1959.

> *This Convention sets out some general obligations for signatories to share information on criminal records, but it is much more limited than ECRIS. There are no timeframes within which Member States would have to respond to requests, and there is no provision for enforcement, so the UK might not receive a response to some requests at all. There is also no set method for sharing information, so the process would be much more laborious and expensive: for example, requests would need to be sent manually, and the information received would not be in a standard format. By contrast, ECRIS is an efficient automated system; uses a standardised format which translates offences to those recognised in the UK; and is governed by strict time frames within which an EU Member State(s) is required to respond. Interpol could potentially be used to issue requests, but it is not designed to deal with the high volumes of requests currently sent through ECRIS,*

> *and would not provide the same capabilities as ECRIS (Scottish Government, 2019, online).*

A solution may be coming from unexpected directions.

At the time of writing this contribution, there are discussions about substantial changes to the system after the attacks in Paris in 2015, to answer the enhanced needs for better screening of non-EU citizens. A substantial improvement in this sense was listed as one of the priorities of the European Agenda on Security.[6]

Another is the so-called European Criminal Records Information System for Third-Country Nationals (ECRIS-TCN), designed to make it easier for the EU's national authorities to obtain the criminal records of non-EU nationals who have been convicted in another Member state(s).

> *The text of the Regulation governing the ECRIS-TCN has been informally agreed between the European Parliament and the Council of the EU and is now awaiting formal adoption by both institutions. ECRIS-TCN will be a centralised database, managed by the European Agency for Large-Scale IT Systems (EU-Lisa), with connections to a national central access point in each Member State. It will hold 'identity information' (biographic data, fingerprints and potentially facial images) that will be accessed by national authorities to ascertain whether people holding citizenship of a non-EU state ('third-country nationals') or stateless persons have a criminal record in any other EU Member State. If a search in the ECRIS-TCN returns a 'hit', the authorities will have to use the existing ECRIS (in operation since 2012) to obtain further information […]. The agreed text sets out*

> *seven possible non-criminal proceedings for which requests can be made (in Article 7(1)),1 although Member States can also decide upon their own purposes, 'if provided under and in accordance with national law'. In this case, they will have to notify the European Commission of these other purposes so that they can be published in the Official Journal of the EU. Three EU agencies – EUROPOL, EUROJUST and the European Public Prosecutor's Office (EPPO) will also be afforded direct access to the system, for various reasons (set out in the annex to this report) (Statewatch, 2019, p. 2).*

An initial impact assessment, which was prepared by the UK Home Office in July 2017 for the Proposal for a Directive and for a Regulation about the exchange of information on third country nationals (TCN) and the ECRIS, and the exercise returned a positive evaluation.

> *ECRIS-TCN provides a more streamlined method of checking whether a TCN has a criminal record overseas. Given that at present ECRIS is used to search for TCNs in only 5% of the cases, and that 30% of ECRIS requests return a criminal record, the expectation is that increased usage of ECRIS to search for TCNs will mean the UK will have a more complete and accurate picture of the EU offending history of TCNs. (…) Although the terms of any future relationship, including financial obligations, are a matter for the negotiations, [this] option allows the UK to maintain our relationship with the EU. By participating in ECRIS-TCN, the UK expresses its desire for future security cooperation. (UK Home Office, 2017, p. 5)*

Whilst ECRIS-TCN will potentially address from the UK perspective the shortcoming of losing access to ECRIS, the enhanced system has raised concerns because it is centralised – instead of the established decentralised approach used by ECRIS – and more privacy-invasive, which The Meijers Committee has described as substantially failing 'to respect the fundamental right to non-discrimination' (Jackson & Davies, 2017, p. 2). The point is not trivial, as calls increase for the ECRIS to uphold ECHR, Art. 8, which requires recording of criminal information to be made in an accurate way, safely stored and disclosed only in proper circumstances (EU Commission, 2017). This new formulation of ECRIS might not be compliant with those provisions. Moreover, if applied as in the present form, ECRIS-TCN may include a potentially discriminatory treatment of dual-citizens.[7]

Due to these considerations, whilst the discussion regarding the implementation of the new system is still long, having the UK treated as a third country rather than as a member may not prove to be an ideal solution.

4.4. CRITICAL POINTS: JUDICIAL COOPERATION

It is generally accepted that one of the key elements of the EU AFSJ *acquis* that UK wants to keep is the European Arrest Warrant (EAW). According to the National Crime Agency, other EU members requested the arrest of 14,279 UK-based suspects in 2015–2016, up from 1,865 in 2004. The UK made 241 such requests in 2015–2016, leading to 150 arrests.[8]

In the total absence of a negotiated arrangement, UK–EU judicial cooperation in this area should turn the clock some 60 years back, to a 'diplomatic/political' cooperative mode; if it would certainly be unlikely that most criminals would escape arrest and execution due to the lack of an EAW-like arrangement; on the other side, it is also certain that the process would become more lengthy and cumbersome in most cases[9]; and could lead to politically sensitive refusals in some, due to the diverging EU and UK laws on fundamental rights.

Some elements to assess what could happen in a post-Brexit UK are given, for example, by the *Melloni* case: the case represents a conflict between, on one side, the Charter of Fundamental Rights of the European Union (CFREU)'s and the EU *acquis'* provisions on surrendering a citizen in execution of a EAW, including those in the Framework Decision 2009/299[10]; and, on the other side, national constitutional rules of requested states, including possibly more generous (towards the accused/convicted) provisions or ECHR-compliant constructions.[11]

The somehow (perhaps apparently) paradoxical outcome of that case,[12] enforcing EU fundamental rights standards rather than more generous national/ECHR ones, makes clear that outside a EU framework both higher-than-EU standards in the requested country, and lower-than-EU ones in the requesting one, will be considered grounds to refuse the surrender of an accused or convicted person.

Both types of contradiction may easily materialise again in cases involving any EU country and post-Brexit UK as a requesting state. Even should the UK maintain a level of protection of fundamental rights consistent with that of the EU, higher-than-EU standards in a requested state could still be enforced to refuse execution – the limitative effect of *Melloni* not being applicable outside the EU framework, and ECHR standards becoming fully applicable at all times *vis-à-vis* the UK, and not just in cases when needed to integrate an incomplete EU discipline.[13]

The UK approach to fundamental rights may also prove an element making future UK–EU negotiations for a EAW-like arrangement much longer,[14] and success less certain – we should be reminded that the corresponding Icelandic and

Norwegian arrangements with the EU imply the continuing relevance of the CJEU case law, if not its direct applicability, in those two countries.

The Home Affairs Committee of the House of Commons also underlined in 2018 that only Iceland and Norway have thus far negotiated cooperative arrangements with the EU approximating the EAW model, and that it took over a decade to finalise the arrangements; and that those arrangements still maintain exceptions for the surrender of own nationals, and in relation to crimes liable in the requested state of being political – which may produce escape avenues for suspected terrorists.[15]

In a post-Brexit 'no-deal' scenario, conclusively, serious doubts exist on whether the EAW, or even a similar instrument negotiated at UK–EU or at multilateral level, may be renegotiated quickly – if at all – due to the changed institutional and legal environment; and still such an arrangement may not work well, due to diverging human rights standards. Meanwhile, however, law enforcement in cross-border cases prosecuted in the UK could be affected significantly.[16]

One, perhaps the only, real option representing something close to a clear, radical zero-sum game – that is, an inevitable trade-off between different, mutually exclusive, non-gradable legal options – is in the area of law enforcement and fundamental rights: 'scrapping the HRA', or departing sharply from its long-established standards, may amount to a political option associated to a totally different security model; thus implying the definitive loss or impossibility of any EAW-like arrangement with the EU.

4. 5. CRITICAL POINTS: THE IRISH LAND BORDER

Brexiteers' agenda is based on restoring British full sovereignty and economic independence. With the existing Backstop agreement, a hard choice will need to be made for the post-Brexit UK: that between remaining in the single market/customs union with the EU to preserve the constitutional integrity of the Kingdom, or restoring the much longed-for independence from the EU at the cost of loosening internal ties with Northern Ireland – introducing a customs border within the UK, in the Irish Sea, thus increasing the possibilities of an eventual Irish reunification, which is constitutionally possible for both the Republic of Ireland[17] and the UK.[18]

After the Brexit Referendum, the Irish Taoiseach (Prime Minister) Enda Kenny claimed during a press conference in Brussels in February 2017 that in case of a reunification of Ireland, the northern part would automatically be part of the EU, under the membership of the Republic of Ireland, as it happened with the German reunification,[19] asking the Council to acknowledge this fact. The European Council acknowledged in April 2017, perhaps stating the obvious, but not without any political impact, that this would be the case.[20]

The UK loosening ties or altogether losing Northern Ireland may, in turn, give momentum to unrest in Scotland – a land of Bremainers as well – with political elements having already asked for a second independence referendum (Bridges, 2019, p. 104).

UK pro-Brexit politicians are proposing a renegotiation/removal of the Backstop arrangement, suggesting that with the entire UK leaving the single market and customs union, even without any trade agreement with the EU, a 'hard' land border in Ireland could still be avoided by making recourse to technological means of control, not necessarily concentrated at the border, keeping the border invisible and soft as much as possible. There is still a vigorous debate on the media on the adequacy of said technological means; details of such technological solutions, however, have not been officially clarified yet.[21]

However difficult it may be to implement this solution, fuzzy, hi-tech, soft, smart, unobtrusive borders – whether in Ireland, in the Irish Sea (possibly including some English or Welsh seaport background land area) or in both – seem to be the only possible condition permitting the UK to leave the EU single market and the customs union without the UK disaggregation, and without installing hard borders in Ireland.

Besides, hi-tech border surveillance is already being introduced in FRONTEX operations, perhaps making possible the extension of some of the related know-how, equipment and operational culture to a different type of border control. A combined use of technology and light or partial regulatory framework may also produce compromise solutions, which could be acceptable for all actors.

It might, of course, at some point become necessary to negotiate a wider political settlement, and/or to enact specific constitutional arrangements, to keep the Kingdom a United one (Kerr, 2019).

The Republic of Ireland may also come under strain in a struggle to maintain both loyalties (to the EU and a Northern Ireland that is still part of the UK), should London somehow negotiate its way out of the Backstop, and either London or Brussels then become willing to introduce an Irish land border, hard enough to be unacceptable for Dublin and/or Belfast. Dublin might have to choose, at some junction, with whom to have common external economic borders and no internal ones, selecting between two mutually exclusive options – basically, aligning its market and custom area with either Schengen or the CTA.

In conclusion, flexibility will be required of both parties in the transition, probably a long one. Uncommon outcomes will doubtlessly be produced: it will not only be that shipping goods from Cardiff to Cork will be different if done via Dublin, or via Belfast: as border lines may become fuzzy or de-compacted in different ways, but also with the help of technology, Northern Ireland will somehow 'pertain', if not 'belong', to both the UK and the EU at the same time – for different but possibly overlapping areas of political and economic governance, in the grey area of a more or less 'temporary' arrangement (or of a lack of it) between the UK and the EU.[22]

The ups-and-downs of politics on either side of the Irish sea, and both parties' historic record of dealing with this issue more or less informally and/or unilaterally – perhaps unequally, sometimes, especially on the UK's side – make any forecasting exercise extremely difficult at this stage.

4.6. A SUMMARY OF THE POSSIBLE SCENARIOS

At the time of the writing of this book, there is still a lack of clarity about the direction the country is going to take upon the repeated defeat of Theresa May's plan in Parliament and her resignation as Premier. Three main post-Brexit scenarios (no-deal, Norway Solution and Swiss Solution) have been analysed in this book, according to different outcomes of the current impasse.

Not all of them are equally possible, but this work does not engage in a likelihood evaluation but only in a qualitative exercise of possible alternatives in the four areas singled out for investigation (intelligence cooperation, information sharing, law enforcement and transnational threats).

A fourth scenario, the revocation of Art. 50, which is always possible albeit unlikely, has not been covered here, even though there would be more to discuss than what it might look like, for the simple fact that the last three years have somehow changed the European outlook, if not at a normative level, at a more subtle, political level.

Advocated by many as the best possible solution both in terms of trade and services and of security cooperation, a Norway-like solution sees the UK remaining in the common market or, at least, in a bespoke framework agreement of a similar kind. Whilst it is allegedly a difficult outcome to achieve – any kind of bespoke solution will take several years to be implemented – this would be, at least, for what concerns the security environment, the best possible outcome. Whilst this would still be changing the type of membership in some of the EU agencies – such as EUROPOL, for instance[23] – it would be still possible to maintain a high level of integration with the current architecture (albeit there are dissenting voices; Bongardt & Torres, 2017).

Any agreement of that kind would present, however, other challenges, in addition to the length and complexity of the negotiations.

Traditionally, the British fear any top-down imposed 'system': the English economy has developed through the centuries as one of the most liberal in the world; the English common law developed piecemeal, a bespoke legal system if we prefer. Whilst the UK is perfectly able to legislate on necessary issues, it still tends to refrain from doing so with a 'framework' approach – which is exactly the odd new thing associated with the HRA 1998.

Framework principles on human rights, CFREU, the very EU legal system and CJEU jurisdiction imply this systematic vision. The British approach is more comfortable with specific arrangements, even small pieces of legislation, precisely drafted; and whatever they do not expressly subscribe to is not supposed to bind them. This is a most distinctive part of their institutional political and legal heritage.

This, in turn, makes a 'Swiss' approach – the third solution – to the relations with the EU a plausible model to look at, neither implying any association with the EU, nor with the

European Free Trade Agreement (EFTA) (and its 'mirror legislation' reproducing the EU one, possibly with the associated jurisdiction or, however, relevance of the CJEU).

A 'Swiss' style piecemeal solution implies, literally, hundreds or thousands of specific agreements that will take years to negotiate (in the case of Switzerland and the EU, it has taken decades to get to the existing regulatory situation). This makes every singular benefit, cooperative measures and arrangement negotiable on a case-by-case basis, rather than on a framework/package basis. It resonates well with the British attitude of retaining national sovereignty, rather than transferring to a different centre of power – precisely what the Swiss put at the base of their rejection of the EFTA treaty at the 1992 referendum.

It must certainly have to do, historically and culturally, with the insularity (one literal; the other cultural and very physically marked by impervious mountains) of both countries. The Kingdom of Norway, on the other side, has a much different institutional and legal tradition of sharing sovereign functions, and other far reaching forms of cooperative arrangements with other national states they cooperate with.

Legal traditions reveal a lot of long-term national inclinations, permitting a better assessment of suitability of solutions through research in comparative law and legal history.

NOTES

1. *Supra*, Chapters II and III.

2. *Supra*, Introduction, Section 1.2.

3. The EU (Withdrawal) Bill, 2017.

4. *Legislating for the United Kingdom's Withdrawal from the European Union*, of 30 March 2017, Cm 9446 (hereinafter: 'the White Paper').

5. The Danish police have a 24-hour 'contact point' to EIS, and therefore they have no such lag as the countries in regime of operational agreements, even though they do not enjoy field access and have no right to vote in EUROPOL meetings.

6. There are many ideas that have been considered in this set of upgrades, for instance, the inclusion of non-EU citizens' fingerprints in the index filter database, the way the EU nationals are searchable. However, the issue with this is that biometric information or, more in general, reliable identification documents are not available even when they are legit, let alone when they are not. In this enhanced system, personal data will be protected by high-security encryption coding software.

7. One of the issues was the disagreement between the EU Parliament and the EU Commission to include or not the fingerprints of dual-nationals, while requiring by default those of third-country ones. It is important to remember that there is no such obligation to fingerprint the EU nationals convicted in their own territories, which the Parliament rejected to avoid discrimination and creating 'two-tiers' of EU citizens. Eventually, the MEPs had them not included, to the dismay of the EU Commission. 'The Commission regrets that the co-legislators have decided to limit the inclusion of fingerprints of convicted third country nationals and dual EU/third country nationals in the ECRIS-TCN system. Since fingerprints are currently the most reliable form of identification of individuals, the Commission regrets these limitations on the inclusion of fingerprints, which in its view will make the ECRIS-TCN system less effective in achieving its aim of ensuring that criminal records information is reliably made available for the purposes of criminal procedures, preventing child abuse, granting licences and other legitimate purposes laid down in national law in line with the Directive'. (*See*: Council document 15701/18 ADD 1, https://data.consilium.europa.eu/doc/document/ST-15701-2018-ADD-1/en/pdf.)

8. Data reported in BBC News, 'UK 'can't keep European Arrest Warrant after Brexit', 19 June 2018, https://www.bbc.com/news/uk-politics-44532500; also see the Home Affairs Committee, Report, item 56.

9. Home Affairs Committee, Report, item 58.

10. Council Framework Decision 2009/299/JHA of 26 February 2009 on procedural rights and mutual recognition of decisions

rendered *in absentia*, amending previous JHA Framework Decisions 2002/584/, 2005/214, 2006/783, 2008/909, 2008/947; OJ L 81, 27 March 2009; ELI: http://data.europa.eu/eli/dec_framw/2009/299/oj

11. CJEU, 26 February 2013, C-399/11, *Melloni* v. *Ministerio Fiscal*, ECLI:EU:C:2013:107.

12. See the discussion above, Section 2.3.

13. As, for example, in CJEU, 26 February 2013, *Åklagaren* v. *Åkerberg Fransson*, and CJEU, 30 May 2013, *Jeremy F.* v. *Premier Ministre*.

14. Home Affairs Committee (2018), Report, item 64.

15. Home Affairs Committee (2018), Report, item 63.

16. Home Affairs Committee, Report, items 63–71.

17. Constitution Art. 3.1.

18. UK Northern Ireland Act 1998, Schedule 1.

19. Boffey, D. (23 February 2017). Irish leader calls for united Ireland provision in Brexit deal. *The Guardian*. Retrieved from https://www.theguardian.com/politics/2017/feb/23/irish-leader-enda-kenny-calls-for-united-ireland-provision-in-brexit-deal. Accessed on 11 June 2019.

20. Macdonald, A. (28 April 2017). EU to say united Ireland would be automatic full member. Reuters. Retrieved from https://www.reuters.com/article/us-britain-eu-ireland/eu-to-say-united-ireland-would-be-automatic-full-member-idUSKBN17U12W. Accessed on 11 June 2019.

21. Some of them are discussed by Katie Daughen, Head of Brexit Policy at the British Irish Chamber of Commerce, in an interview of 1 June 2018 to Abigail Beall of Wired, available online; the interviewees, however, concluded that said technologies were still inadequate to face the heavy challenges of the devised soft Irish land border. https://www.wired.co.uk/article/irish-border-brexit-tech.

22. This would not be entirely uncommon: cases of co-existing multiple governance structures and legal pluralism are known in geography and history, often made possible by de-compacting jurisdictional borders to make them movable according to the different subject-matter or persons to be regulated – irrespective

sometimes of whether the relevant different institutional systems agree, disagree or even are indifferent to this fuzzy condition. See, for example, on the co-existence of both the German Empire and the Byzantine one in Southern Italy for some 150 years between the ninth and the tenth centuries (Cortese, 2000, p. 171 & 179–181; Lamma, 1968, pp. 231–337).

CONCLUSIONS

At the times of writing, the destiny of the UK is still much in doubt; between the former PM Theresa May's deal being rejected three times by the Commons in a decisive way and another clear-cut rejection by the Parliament to 'crash out of the EU' without a deal, the future has never looked more uncertain.

However, things are looking increasingly orientated in the sense of a no-deal, which means the terms of the UK leaving the European Union (EU) remain undefined, security included. Whatever the kind of agreement is negotiated afterwards, it will require a transition period to be implemented through further long-term agreements to be negotiated.

In the meantime, the forces at work discussed in Chapter 4, and that have pushed towards this 'natural' integration of the different institutions of the sector – the terrorist threat first and foremost, and more in general, transnational crime – will keep working their own way, producing consequences intended and not.

In a more general perspective, it is possible that further centralisation at the EU level will be fostered exactly by the fact of the UK leaving the EU, and therefore, by the EU losing the substantial intelligence expertise of the UK in this sector.

> *In concrete terms, a coalition of EU member states could embark on the path of closer cooperation in*

> *the field of Common Foreign and Security Policy (CFSP) under Article 329 of the Treaty on the Functioning of the European Union (TFEU). Since the EU-SIAC is already regarded as a component of the CFSP and the EEAS, a deepening of these structures would not have to come into conflict with national prerogatives in the area of national security (Art. 4 (2) TEU). (Bossong, 2018, p. 3)*

Similar, apparently paradoxical, outcomes have also been predicted by analysts with relation to European defence matters (Ferreira Nunes, 2017).

Whatever the scenario that is going to materialise, there are reasons for optimism especially what concerns the intelligence sector, both in terms of cooperation and information sharing. Intelligence sharing does exist in Europe, and traditionally has not taken place at EU centralised level, but at a bilateral level instead.

Even after the constitution of SITCEN/INCENT, the sector has remained a matter firmly in the hands of Member state(s), which still 'own' the intelligence shared at central level. There is reason to believe that this is not going to be affected by Brexit, even if, and when, an EU centralised, full-fledged service, eventually appears (upon modification of the Lisbon Treaty). There are many, on both sides of the Channel, who believe that the idea of an EU Intelligence Agency on the typology of CIA does not serve any real interest, regardless of Brexit. If any, the collective effort should be steered in order to make the existing information sharing more reliable and efficient, especially under a terrorism-containment perspective.

There are, however, also reasons for concern, which are going to affect particularly the law-enforcement sector, which, on the other hand, is far more centralised than the intelligence world even though they often are after the same targets (e.g., terrorist threats).

This duality and difference in consequences for the different sectors of security have been acknowledged even by senior officials, such as Rob Wainwright, EUROPOL Chief, during a Parliament Hearing.

> *On counter-terrorism, I think that it is fair to say that the UK's primary interests have been leveraged through the intelligence community and that co-operation, but on fighting organised crime – as your question suggests – the balance has been more from benefits from the EU systems of co-operation, for example on the UK's bid to advance the cause of fighting modern slavery across Europe, and migrant smuggling, and cybercrime in particular. (House of Commons, 2017, online)*

A no-deal Brexit will see the UK resigning its full membership from organisations like EUROPOL, to which it has contributed so much to shape, and losing the use of highly efficient instruments, such as EAW or ECRIS, at least in the short term. It remains to be seen which kind of solution will be available in terms of international cooperation to offset the need of finding analogous devices in the long run.

REFERENCES

Alì, A. (2019). The challenges of a sanctions machine: Some reflections on the legal issues of EU restrictive measures in the field of common foreign security policy. In L. Antoniolli, L. Bonatti, & C. Ruzza (Eds.), *Highs and lows of European integration: Sixty years after the treaty of Rome* (pp. 49–62). Berlin: Springer.

Alkema, E. A., van der Hulle, R., & van der Hulle, R. (2015). Safeguard rules in the European legal order: The relationship between art. 53 of the European Convention on Human Rights and art. 53 of the Charter of Fundamental Rights of the European Union. *Human Rights Law Journal, 35*(1), 8.

Angelescu, I., & Trainer, F. (2018). *10,000 border guards for Frontex: why the EU risks conflated expectations*. European Policy Center. Retrieved from https://www.epc.eu/documents/uploads/pub_8745_frontex.pdf?doc_id=2048

Antoniolli, L., Bonatti, L., & Ruzza, C. (Eds.). (2019). *Highs and lows of European integration: Sixty years after the treaty of Rome*. Berlin: Springer.

Arpaia, V. (2019). *Tempo di muri: Un mondo diviso: da Berlino a Trump*. Milan: Luni.

Arroyo Jiménez, M. (2011). Sobre la primera cuestión prejudicial planteada por el Tribunal Constitucional – Bases, contenido y consecuencias. *Madrid: Universidad Complutense.*

Atanassov, N. (2018). *Revision of the Schengen information system for border checks*. European Parliamentary Research Service. Retrieved from http://www.europarl.europa.eu/RegData/etudes/BRIE/2017/599341/EPRS_BRI(2017)599341_EN.pdf. Accessed on October 18, 2018.

Baciu, C.-A., & Doyle, J. (eds.) (2019). *Peace, security and defence cooperation in post-Brexit Europe: Risks and opportunities*. Berlin: Springer.

Baker, N. (2003). National security versus civil liberties. *Presidential Studies Quarterly*, *33*(3), 547–567.

Bendiek, A. (2006). *EU strategy on counter-terrorism. Steps towards a Coherent Network Policy*. SWP Research Paper. SWP, Berlin.

Benedicto, A. R., & Brunet, P. (2018, September). *Building walls: Fear and securitization in the European Union*. Report 35. Centre Delàs d'estudis per la pau, Barcelona.

Best, M. (2013). The ethnic Russian minority: A problematic issue in the Baltic States. *Germanic & Slavic Studies in Review (GSSR)*, *2*(1), 33–41.

Biondi, F., & Gonçalves Raposo, I. (2016). The impact of Brexit on Northern Ireland: A first look. Retrieved from http://bruegel.org/2016/12/the-impact-of-brexit-on-northern-ireland-a-first-look/. Accessed on December 22, 2016.

Blunkett, D. (2004). Counter-terrorism powers: Reconciling security and liberty in an open society. Discussion Paper presented to the UK Parliament by the Secretary of State for the Home Department. Retrieved from http://www.statewatch.org/news/2004/feb/uk-CT-discussion-paper.pdf. Accessed on May 25, 2019.

Boer, M. D., & Monar, J. (2002). Keynote article: 11 September and the challenge of global terrorism to the EU as a security actor. *Journal of Common Market Studies, 40*(Supplement 1), 11–28.

Bongardt, A., & Torres, F. (2017). Sobre a lógica e termos da saída do reino unido da União Europeia. *Nação e Defesa, 147*, 18.

Bossong, R. (2018). *Intelligence support for EU security policy. Options for enhancing the flow of information and political oversight*. SWP Discussion Paper #5. SWP, Berlin.

Bridges, R. (2019). Il confine irlandese è il cuore del Brexit [The Irish Border is at the Heart of Brexit]. Limes – Rivista Italiana di Geopolitica (pp. 99–104). 5/2019, La questione Britannica.

Brière, Chloé, Cooperation of Europol and Eurojust with External Partners in the Fight Against Crime: What are the Challenges Ahead? (2018, January 15). DCU Brexit Institute Working Paper No. 1–2018. Retrieved from https://ssrn.com/abstract=3102394 or http://dx.doi.org/10.2139/ssrn.3102394. Accessed on December 23, 2018.

Cortese, E. (2000). *Le grandi linee della storia giuridica medieval*. Rome: Il Cigno.

Cosio, R., & Foglia, R. (Eds.). (2013). *Il diritto europeo nel dialogo delle Corti*. Milan: Giuffré.

Craig, P. (2013). The nature of unreasonableness review. *Current Legal Problems, 66*, 131–167.

Cruz, C. F. (2018). A comunidade de intelligence contraterrorista da União Europeia: Evolução e desafios face à perspetiva do Brexit. Master's Dissertation, University of Minho, Braga, Portugal.

Daehnhardt, P. (2017). O reino unido e a alemanha após o "Brexit": As trajetórias inversas de duas potências Europeias. *Nação e Defesa*, *147*, 92.

de Mars, S., Murray, C., O'Donoghue, A., & Warwick, B. (2018). Discussion Paper on the Common Travel Area, the Irish Human Rights and Equality Commission and the Northern Ireland Human Rights Commission. Retrieved from http://www.nihrc.org/publication/detail/discussion-paper-on-the-common-travel-area; https://www.ihrec.ie/documents/discussion-paper-on-the-common-travel-area/

Dornan, M. (2011). *Security vs. liberty? Is there a trade off?* E-International Relations Publishing. Retrieved from https://www.e-ir.info/2011/06/23/security-vs-liberty-is-there-a-trade-off/. Accessed on April 2, 2019.

Doyle, J., & Connoly, E. (2017). Brexit and the Northern Ireland question. In F. Fabbrini (Ed.), *The law & politics of Brexit* (pp. 139–159). Oxford: Oxford University Press.

Dragu, T. (2011, February). Is there a trade-off between security and liberty? Executive bias, privacy protections, and terrorism prevention. *The American Political Science Review*, *105*(1), 64–78.

Fabbrini, F. (Ed.). (2017). *The law & politics of Brexit.* Oxford: Oxford University Press

Feldman, D. (1999). Proportionality and the Human Rights Act 1998. In E. Ellis (Ed.), *The principles of proportionality in the laws of Europe* (pp. 117–144). London: Hart Publishing.

Ferreira Nunes, I. (2017). O referendo britânico e a segurança e defesa Europeia. *Nação e Defesa*, *147*, 112.

Gamble, A. (2019). La gran bretagna ha perso l'Europa e non ha ancora trovato un impero. Limes – Rivista Italiana di Geopolitica. 5/2019 (pp. 41–46), La questione Britannica.

Gaspar, C. (2017). A crise da segurança Europeia. *Nação e Defesa*, *147*, 61.

Gofas, A. (2012). The terrorism-democracy nexus and the trade-off between security and civil liberties. In N. Tzifakis (Ed.), *International politics in times of change*. Athens, Greece: The Konstantinos Karamanlis Institute for Democracy Series on European and International Affairs. doi:10.1007/978-3-642-21955-9_17

Groussot, X. (2006). *General principles of community law*. Groeningen: Europa Law Publishing.

Hayes, K. (2017). "Brexit": Consequences for the EU, NATO and Portugal. *Nação e Defesa*, *147*, 12.

Hill, C. (2019). *The future of British foreign policy: Security and diplomacy in a world after Brexit*. Cambridge: Polity Press.

Hoffman, D., & Rowe, J. (2010). *Human rights in the UK: An introduction to the Human Rights Act 1998* (3rd ed.). Harlow: Pearson Education.

Jackson A. M., & Davies, G. L. (2017). Making the case for ECRIS: Post 'Brexit' sharing of criminal records information between the European Union and United Kingdom. *The International Journal of Evidence & Proof*. https://doi.org/10.1177/1365712717692813. Accessed on December 23, 2019.

Kendall, R. E. (2004). Financial crime, terror and subversion. *Journal of Financial Crime*, *11*(4), 363–365. https://doi.org/10.1108/13590790410809356

Keohane, D. (2008). The absent friend: EU foreign policy and counter-terrorism. *Journal of Common Market Studies*, *46*(1), 125–146.

Kerr, M. (2019). La linea del Brexit nel mare d'Irlanda. Limes – Rivista Italiana di Geopolitica. 5/2019 (pp. 111–115), La questione Britannica.

La Spina, A. (2014). The fight against the Italian Mafia. In L. Paoli (ed.), *The Oxford Handbook of Organised Crime*. Oxford: Oxford University Press.

Lamma, P. (1968). Il problema dei due imperi e dell'Italia meridionale nel giudizio delle fonti leterarie dei secoli IX e X. In *Oriente e Occidente nell'altro medioevo – Studi storici sulle due civiltà*. Padua: Antenore.

Larkin, C. (2019). In Irlanda il passato non passa mai. Limes – Rivista Italiana di Geopolitica. 5/2019 (pp. 105–109), La questione Britannica.

Lonardo, L. (2018, April 27). EU common foreign and security policy after Brexit: A security and defence treaty for the 'deep and special partnership'. Brexit Institute – Working Paper No. 4. Retrieved from https://ssrn.com/abstract=3169898 or http://dx.doi.org/10.2139/ssrn.3169898. Accessed on December 12, 2019.

Mac Flynn, P. (2016, April). *The economic implications of Brexit for Northern Ireland*. NERI Working paper 2016/No 35. Nevin Economic Research Institute. Retrieved from www.NERInstitute.net

Mackinder, H. (1904, April). The geographical pivot of history. *The Geographical Journal*, *XXIII*(4), 421–444.

Mariani, P. (2018). *Lasciare l'unione Europea*. Milan: Egea.

Martill, B., & Staiger, U. (2018). *Brexit and beyond: Rethinking the futures of Europe*. London: UCL Press.

Mathisen, G. (2010). Nordic cooperation and the European arrest warrant: Intra-Nordic extradition. *The Nordic Arrest Warrant and Beyond*, *79*, 1.

McGlynn, P., & Garner, G. (2019). *Intelligence analysis fundamentals*. Boca Ratos, FL: CRC Press.

Müller-Wille, B. (2004b). Building a European intelligence community in response to terrorism. *European Security Review*, *22*, 3–4.

Nanula, G. (2009). *La lotta alla mafia: Strumenti giuridici, strutture di coordinamento, legislazione vigente*. Milan: Giuffré

Nguyen, T. (2017). The effectiveness of white-collar crime enforcement: Evidence from the war on terror. Stanford PhD dissertation. Retrieved from https://ssrn.com/abstract=3117719

Nomikos, J. M. (2005). A European Union intelligence service for confronting terrorism. *International Journal of Intelligence and Counterintelligence*, *18*(2),191–203.

Paladini, S., & Castellucci, I. (2017). Intelligence and European security in the aftermath of Brexit: An Italian perspective. *Journal of Intelligence History*, *16*(2), 87–90.

Paoli, L (2007). Mafia and organised crime in Italy: The unacknowledged success of law enforcement. *West European Politics*, *30*(4), 854–880.

Parks, L. (2019). All quiet on the Brexit front? UK Civil Society Before and after the UK's referendum on membership of the EU. In L. Antoniolli, L. Bonatti, & C. Ruzza (Eds.), *Highs and lows of European integration: Sixty years after the treaty of Rome* (pp. 105–120). Berlin: Springer.

Pereira Coutinho, F. (2017). A Caminho do "Brexit" ou do "Breversal"? A reversibilidade doprocesso de secessão de estados-membros na União Europeia. *Nação e Defesa*,*147*, 39.

Pierce, N. (2019). L'anglosfera è un'illusione geopolitica. Limes – Rivista Italiana di Geopolitica. 5/2019 (pp. 151–156), La questione Britannica.

Posner, E. A., & Vermeule, A. (2007). *Terror in the balance: Security, liberty, and the courts*. New York, NY: Oxford University Press.

Radin, A. (2017). *Hybrid warfare in the Baltics: Threats and potential responses*. Rand Corporation. Retrieved from https://www.rand.org/content/dam/rand/pubs/research_reports/RR1500/RR1577/RAND_RR1577.pdf

Rodrigues Viana, V. (2017). Editorial. *Nação e Defesa*, *147*, 5.

Ryder, N. (2017). *The financial war on terrorism: A review of counterterrorim financial strategies since 2001*. Abingdon-on-Thames: Routledge.

Salvatore, V. (2016). The relation between Switzerland and the European Union: Historical evolution and current legal framework. In V. Salvatore (Ed.), *The free movement of persons between Switzerland and the European Union* (pp. 1–10). Turin: Giappichelli.

Scanlan, G. (2005). The war on terror: Future trends. *Journal of Financial Crime*, *12*(2), 104–111. https://doi.org/10.1108/13590790510624927

Schermers, H. G. (2000). Human rights as general principles of law. In U. Bernitz & J. Nergelius (Eds.), *General principles of European community law* (p. 61). The Hague: Kluwer.

Sergi, A. (2013). Structure versus activity. Policing organised crime in Italy and in the UK, Distance and convergence. *Policing*, 1–10. Retrieved from http://www.policing.oxfordjournals.org, doi:10.1093/police/pat033

Sergi, A. (2017). *From mafia to organised crime: A comparative analysis of policing models*. Basingstoke: Palgrave Macmillan.

Sevon, L. (1992). The EEA judicial system and the supreme courts of the EFTA states. *European Journal of International Law*, *3*, 329–340

Silberstein, S. (2004). *War of worlds: Language, politics and 9/11*. London: Routledge.

Sirena, P. (2016). La giurisprudenza della Corte europea dei diritti dell'uomo e l'art. 6 del Trattato sull'Unione europea. La nuova giurisprudenza civile commentata, XXXII, 1, 119.

Spielmann, D. (2017). The Judicial Dialogue between the European Court of Justice and the European Court of Human RightsOr how to remain good neighbours after the Opinion 2/13. Conference paper. Brussels, 27 March 2017. Retrieved from http://www.fp7-frame.eu/wp-content/uploads/2017/03/ECHRCJUEdialog.BRUSSELS.final_.pdf

Spykeman, N. J. (1944). *The geography of the peace*. New York, NY: Harcourt, Brace and Company.

Srirangam, V. (2016, Autumn). A difference in kind. Proportionality and Wednesbury. *IALS Student Law Review*, *4*(1), 46–66.

Tesauro, G. (2013). Relazioni tra corte costituzionale e corte di giustizia. In R. Cosio & R. Foglia (Eds.), *Il diritto europeo nel dialogo delle Corti* (p. 11). Milan: Giuffré.

Tinsley, A. (2012). Note on the reference in case C-399/11 Melloni. *New Journal of European Criminal Law*, *3*(1), 19.

van de Heyning, C. (2011). No place like home – Discretionary space for the domestic protection of fundamental rights. In P. Popelier, C. Van de Heyning, & P. Van Nuffel (Eds.), *Human rights protection in the European legal order: The interaction between the European and the national courts* (pp. 65–96). Cambridge: Intersentia.

Vermeule, A. (2011). *Security and liberty: Critiques of the Tradeoff Thesis*. Harvard Law School Public Law & Legal Theory Working Paper Series Paper No. 11–19. Retrieved from http://ssrn.com/abstract=1888334

Walsh, J. I. (2006). Intelligence-sharing in the European Union: Institutions are not enough. *Journal of Common Market Studies*, *44*(3), 625–643.

Walzer, M. (2006). *Just and unjust wars: A moral argument with historical illustrations*. New York, NY: Basic Books.

Widmann, A. M. (2002). Article 53: Undermining the impact of the charter of fundamental rights. *Columbia Journal of European Law*, *8*(2), 342.

Włodarska-Frykowska, A. (2016). Ethnic Russian minority in Estonia. *International Studies – Interdisciplinary Political and Cultural Journal*, *18*(2/2016), 153–164.

Ziccardi Capaldo, G. (2011). Il principio di buona fede nell'esecuzione dei trattati – il caso Battisti: Un esempio emblematico di mala fides. In T. Vassalli di Dachenhausen (Ed.), *Atti del convegno in memoria di Luigi Sico* (pp. 509–534). Napoli: Editoriale Scientifica.

Relevant Cases

EEC – EC – EU Cases

CJEC, 17 December 1970, C-11/70, *Internationale Handgesellschaft mbH* v. *Einfuhr- und Vorrastelle fur getreide und Futtermittel*; European Court Reports, 1970-01125.

CJEC, 14 May 1974, C-4/73, *Nold v. European Commission*, European Court Reports 1974-00491.

CJEC, 28 October 1975, C-36/75, *Rutili c. Ministre de l'Intérieur*, European Court Reports 1975-01219.

CJEC, 13 December 1979, C-44/79, *Hauer* v. *Land Rheinland-Pfalz*, European Court Reports 1979-03727.

CJEU, 3 September 2008, Joined Cases C-402/05/ P and C-415/04 P, *Yassin Abdullah Kadi - Al Barakaat International Foundation v. Council of the European Union and Commission of the European Communities*, ECLI:EU:C:2008:461.

CJEU, 26 February 2013a, C-399/11, *Melloni* v. *Ministerio Fiscal*, ECLI:EU:C:2013:107.

CJEU, 26 February 2013b, C-617/10, *Åklagaren* v. *Åkerberg Fransson*, ECLI:EU:C:2013:105.

CJEU, 30 May 2013, C-168/13 PPU, *Jeremy F.* v. *Premier Ministre*, ECLI:EU:C:2013:358.

CJEU, 27 May 2019, preliminary ruling in joint cases C-508/18,*OG*, and C 89/19 PPU, *PI*, ECLI:EU:C:2019:456.

CJEU, Grand Chamber, 18 December 2007, C-77/05, *United Kingdom* v. *Council*, ECLI:EU:C:2007:803.

Opinion of Advocate General Bot, delivered on 2 October 2012, Case C-399/11, *Melloni* v. *Ministerio Fiscal*, ECLI:EU:C:2012:600.

Opinion of Advocate General Bot, delivered on 19 March 2013, Joined Cases C-584/10 P, C-593/10 P and C-595/10 P, *European Commission, Council of the European Union, United Kingdom of Great Britain and Northern Ireland v Yassin Abdullah Kadi*, ECLI:EU:C:2013:176.

Opinion of Advocate General Trstenjak delivered on 10 July 2007, Case C-77/05, *United Kingdom v. Council*, ECLI:EU:C:2007:419.

UK Cases

Associated Provincial Picture Houses Ltd v. *Wednesbury Corp.* (1948) 1 KB 223.

de Freitas v. *Permanent Secretary of Ministry of Agriculture, Fisheries, Lands and Housing* (1999) 1 AC69.

Huang v. *Secretary of State for the Home Department* (2007) UKHL 11, (2007) 2 A.C. 167.

Kennedy v. *Charity Commission* (2014) UKSC 20.

Miller (2016) EWHC 2768 5, 50.

Pham v. *Secretary of State for the Home Department* (2015) UKSC 19, W.L.R. 1591.

R. (Razgar) v. *Secretary of State for the Home Department* (2004) UKHL 27, (2004) 2 A.C. 368, (20).

Other Cases

Bunderverfassungsgericht, 29 May 1974, *Solange I*, in BverfGE 37, 271.

Bunderverfassungsgericht, 22 October 1986, *Solange II*, in BVerfGE 73, 39.

Bunderverfassungsgericht, 12 October 1993, *Maastricht*, BVerfGE 89, 155..

Conseil d'État, 11–18 March 2005, No. 273714.

Cour de Cassation, 13 October 2004, No. 04–84.470.

European Court of Human Rights, 12 December 2006, No. 28796/05.

EU and European Basic Instruments

CFREU, Charter of Fundamental Rights of the European Union. OJ C 326, 26.10.2012, 391–407. Retrieved from http://data.europa.eu/eli/treaty/char_2012/oj

ECHR, European Convention on Human Rights signed in Rome on 4 November, 1950. Consolidated text. Retrieved from https://echr.coe.int/Documents/Convention_ENG.pdf

TEU, Treaty on the European Union. Consolidated version. OJ C 326, 26.10.2012, 13–390; ELI. Retrieved from http://data.europa.eu/eli/treaty/teu_2012/oj

TFEU, Treaty on the Functioning of the European Union. Consolidated version. OJ C 326, 26.10.2012, 47–390; ELI. Retrieved from http://data.europa.eu/eli/treaty/tfeu_2012/oj

The EEA Agreement: Agreement on the European Economic Area, OJ L 1, 3.1.1994, 3–522. Consolidated version. Retrieved from https://eur-lex.europa.eu/legal-content/EN/TXT/?uri=CELEX:01994A0103(01)-20190207

The Schengen acquis – Agreement between the Governments of the States of the Benelux Economic Union, the Federal Republic of Germany and the French Republic on the gradual abolition of checks at their common borders, OJ L 239, 22.9.2000, 13–18.

List of Relevant Statutes

UK Statutes

The EU (Withdrawal) Act, 2018.

The Human Rights Act, 1998.

The Northern Ireland Act, 1998.

EU Instruments – Regulations, Council Framework Decision, etc.

EAW

2002/584/JHA: Council Framework Decision of 13 June 2002 on the European Arrest Warrant and the surrender procedures between Member States; OJ L 190/1, 18 July 2002.

Council Decision of 27 November 2014 determining certain consequential and transitional arrangements concerning the cessation of the participation of the United Kingdom of Great Britain and Northern Ireland in certain acts of the Union in the field of police cooperation and judicial cooperation in criminal matters adopted before the entry into force of the Treaty of Lisbon. OJ L 343/11, 27 November 2014,

Council Framework Decision 2009/299/JHA of 26 February 2009 on procedural rights and mutual recognition of decisions rendered in absentia, amending previous JHA Framework Decisions 2002/584/, 2005/214, 2006/783, 2008/909, 2008/947; OJ L 81, 27 March 2009.

EEAS

Council Decision (2010/427/EU) of 26 July 2010, establishing the organisation and functioning of the European External Action Service, OJ L201/30, 3 August 2010.

ENISA

Regulation (EU) 2019/881 of the European Parliament and of the Council of 17 April 2019 on ENISA (the European Union Agency for Cybersecurity) and on information and communications technology cybersecurity certification and repealing Regulation (EU) No 526/2013 (Cybersecurity Act), OJ L 151, 7.6.2019, pp. 15–69

Directive (EU) 2016/679 of 6 July 2016, concerning measures for a high common level of security of network and information systems across the Union, OJ L 194, 19.7.2016, p.1

Reg (EC) 460/2004 Regulation (EC) No 460/2004 of the European Parliament and of the Council of 10 March 2004 establishing the European Network and Information Security Agency, OJ L 77, 13.3.2004, p. 1–11

EUROJUST-EPPO

Council Decision No. 2002/187/JHA, OJ L 63/1, 6 March 2002; amended by Council Decision no. 2003/659/JHA, OJ L 245, 29.9.2003, pp. 44–45.

Council Regulation 2017/1939 adopted by the JHA Council of 12 October 2017 implementing enhanced cooperation on the establishment of the European Public Prosecutor's Office ('the EPPO'), OJ L 283, 31.10.2017, pp. 1–71.

Regulations (EU) 2018/1727 replacing and repealing Council Decision 2002/187/JHA of 14 November 2018, OJ L 295/138, 21 November 2018.

EUROPOL

Regulation (EU) 2016/794 of the European Parliament and of the Council of 11 May 2016, on Europol, replacing Council Decisions 2009/371/JHA, 2009/934/JHA, 2009/935/JHA, 2009/936/JHA and 2009/968/JHA; OJ L 35/53, 24 May 2016.

FRONTEX-EUROSUR

Council Regulation (EC) 2007/2004 of 26 October 2004, OJ L 49, 25 November 2004.

Regulation (EU) 1052/2013 of 22 October 2013, establishing the European Border Surveillance System (Eurosur), OJ L 295/11, 6 November 2013.

Regulation (EU) 656/2014 of 15 May 2014, establishing rules for the surveillance of the external sea borders in the context of operational cooperation coordinated by the European Agency for the Management of Operational Cooperation at the External Borders of the Member States of the European Union, OJ L 189/93, 27 June 2014.

Regulation (EU) 2016/1624 of 14 September 2016 on the European Border and Coast Guard, OJ L 251, 16 September 2016, 1.

PROTECTION OF SENSITIVE DATA

Regulation (EU) 2018/1725 of the European Parliament and of the Council of 23 October 2018 on the protection of natural persons with regard to the processing of personal data by the Union institutions, bodies, offices and agencies and on the free movement of such data, and repealing Regulation (EC) No 45/2001 and Decision No 1247/2002/EC, OJ L 295, 21.11.2018, p. 39–98

Commission Decision (EU, Euratom) 2015/443 of 13 March 2015 on Security in the Commission, *OJ L 72, 17.3.2015, p. 41–52.*

Commission Decision (EU, Euratom) 2015/444 of 13 March 2015 on the security rules for protecting EU classified information, *OJ L 72, 17.3.2015, p. 53–88.*

SIS II – ECRIS

Council Decision 2001/886/JHA of 6 December 2001 on the development of the second generation Schengen Information System (SIS II), OJ L 328, 13.12.2001, pp. 1–3.

Council Decision 2007/533/JHA of 12 June 2007 on the establishment, operation and use of the second generation Schengen Information System (SIS II), OJ L 205, 7.8.2007, pp. 63–84.

Council Decision 2009/316/JHA of 6 April 2009 on the establishment of the European Criminal Records Information System (ECRIS) in application of Article 11 of Framework Decision 2009/315/JHA OJ L 93, 7.4.2009, pp. 33–48.

Council Framework Decision 2009/315/JHA of 26 February 2009 on the organisation and content of the exchange of information extracted from the criminal record between Member States OJ L 93, 7.4.2009, pp. 23–32.

Regulation (EC) No 1986/2006 of the European Parliament and of the Council of 20 December 2006 regarding access to the Second Generation Schengen Information System (SIS II) by the services in the Member States responsible for issuing vehicle registration certificates, OJ L 381, 28.12.2006, pp. 1–3.

Regulation (EC) No 1987/2006 of the European Parliament and of the Council of 20 December 2006 on the establishment, operation and use of the second generation Schengen Information System (SIS II), OJ L 381, 28.12.2006, pp. 4–23.

Regulation (EU) 2016/399 of the European Parliament and of the Council of 9 March 2016 on a Union Code on the rules governing the movement of persons across borders (Schengen Borders Code), OJ L 77/1, 23 March 2016, pp. 1–52.

Regulation (EU) 2018/1860 of the European Parliament and of the Council of 28 November 2018 on the use of the Schengen Information System for the return of illegally staying third-country nationals, OJ L 312, 7.12.2018, pp. 1–13.

Regulation (EU) 2018/1861 of the European Parliament and of the Council of 28 November 2018 on the establishment, operation and use of the Schengen Information System (SIS) in the field of border checks, and amending the Convention implementing the Schengen Agreement, and amending and repealing Regulation (EC) No 1987/2006, OJ L 312, 7.12.2018, pp. 14–55.

Regulation (EU) 2018/1862 of the European Parliament and of the Council of 28 November 2018 on the establishment, operation and use of the Schengen Information System (SIS) in the field of police cooperation and judicial cooperation in criminal matters, amending and repealing Council Decision 2007/533/JHA, and repealing Regulation (EC) No 1986/2006 of the European Parliament and of the Council and Commission Decision 2010/261/EU, OJ L 312, 7.12.2018, pp. 56–106.

Other Documents

EU

Council of the European Union. (2005a, November 11). Policy recommendations on counter-terrorism: Anatomy of a terrorist network, 14316/05, Brussels.

Council of the European Union. (2005b, November 28). Report on Support from Member States Security and Intelligence Services to SITCEN, 15010/05, Brussels.

Council of the European Union. (2007f, March 12). Overview of SitCen reports and Political Recommendations, 7261/07 RESTREINT, Brussels.

Council Conclusions. (2010). On the creation and implementation of a EU policy cycle for organised and serious international crime (doc. 15358/10).

Draft Agreement on the withdrawal of the United Kingdom of Great Britain and Northern Ireland from the European Union and the European Atomic Energy Community, as agreed at negotiators' level on 14 November 2018. Retrieved from https://ec.europa.eu/commission/publications/draft-agreement-withdrawal-united-kingdom-great-britain-and-northern-ireland-european-union-and-european-atomic-energy-community-agreed-negotiators-level-14-november-2018_en

EU INTCEN Fact Sheet. (2018). Factsheet-PUBLIC-UE-05022015. Retrieved from http://statewatch.org/news/2016/may/eu-intcen-factsheet.pdf. Accessed on December 23, 2018.

European Commission. (2017). Analytical Supporting Document, Accompanying the document, Proposal for a Regulation of the European Parliament and of the Council establishing a centralised system for the identification of Member States holding conviction information on third country nationals and stateless people (TCN) to supplement and support the European Criminal Records Information System (ECRISTCN system) and amending Regulation (EU) No. 1077/2011. Retrieved from https://ec.europa.eu/info/sites/info/files/analytical_supporting_document_accompanying_the_proposal_2.pdf. Accessed on Dec. 23, 2018.

European External Action Service. (2012). Organizational chart. Retrieved from http://www.eeas.europa.eu, eu/background/docs/organisation_en.pdf. Accessed on November 5, 2014.

European Parliament, Briefing No. 32, The European Economic Area (EEA) and the enlargement of the European Union, 1998.

Retrieved from http://www.europarl.europa.eu/enlargement/briefings/32a2_en.htm. Accessed on April 10, 2019.

European Parliament resolution of 12 Feb. 2019, on the implementation of the Charter of Fundamental Rights of the European Union in the EU institutional framework. Retrieved from http://www.europarl.europa.eu/doceo/document/TA-8-2019-0079_EN.html

Political Declaration Setting Out the Framework for the Future Relationship between the European Union and the United Kingdom. Retrieved from https://assets.publishing.service.gov.uk/government/uploads/system/uploads/attachment_data/file/759021/25_November_Political_Declaration_setting_out_the_framework_for_the_future_relationship_between_the_European_Union_and_the_United_Kingdom__.pdf

UK

Explainer for the agreement on the withdrawal of the United Kingdom of Great Britain and Northern Ireland from the European Union, 14 November 2018. Retrieved from https://assets.publishing.service.gov.uk/government/uploads/system/uploads/attachment_data/file/759020/14_November_Explainer_for_the_agreement_on_the_withdrawal_of_the_United_Kingdom_of_Great_Britain_and_Northern_Ireland_from_the_European_Union.pdf

Explainer for the Political Declaration setting out the framework for the future relationship between the United Kingdom and the European Union, 25 November 2018. Retrieved from https://assets.publishing.service.gov.uk/government/uploads/system/uploads/attachment_data/file/759022/25_November_Explainer_for_the_Political_Declaration_setting_out_the_framework_for_the_future_ relationship_between_the_European_Union_and_the_United_Kingdom___1_.pdf

House of Commons. (2017). Oral evidence: EU policing and security issues, HC 806. Tuesday, 7 March 2017.

House of Commons, Home Affairs Committee. (2015). Retrieved from http://www.parliament.uk/business/committees/committees-a-z/commons-select/home-affairs-committee/inquiries/parliament-2015/inquiry12/ retrieved. Accessed on December 23, 2019.

House of Commons, Home Affairs Committee. (2018). Report of an inquiry on UK-EU security cooperation after Brexit, 21 March 2018, item 69. Retrieved from https://publications.parliament.uk/pa/cm201719/cmselect/cmhaff/635/63507.htm

House of Commons, Northern Ireland Affairs Committee. (2018). The land border between Northern Ireland and Ireland – Second Report of Session 2017–2019, 16 March 2018.

House of Lords, EU Committee. (2008). Frontex: the EU external borders agency – 9th Report of Session 2007–2008. 5 March 2008. Retrieved from https://publications.parliament.uk/pa/ld200708/ldselect/ldeucom/60/60.pdf. Accessed on March 5, 2008.

Memorandum of the UK Government. (2018). European Union (Withdrawal) Bill – European Convention on Human Rights – Memorandum by the Department for Exiting the EU of 18 January 2018. Retrieved from http://www.devolutionclub.it/wp-content/uploads/2018/01/European-Union-ECHR-Memorandum.pdf

NPCC. (2019). New unit ready to help UK police cooperate with the EU in event of no deal exit. Retrieved from https://news.npcc.police.uk/releases/new-unit-ready-to-help-uk-police-cooperate-with-the-eu-in-event-of-no-deal-exit. Accessed on March 23, 2019.

Scottish Government. (2019). Scotland's Place in Europe: Security, judicial co-operation and law enforcement. Retrieved from https://www.gov.scot/publications/scotlands-place-europe-security-judicial-co-operation-law-enforcement/pages/5/. Accessed on January 14, 2019.

Shapcott, W. (2010, December 6). Witness transcripts at House of Lords Select Committee on the European Union, 'Inquiry on EU Internal Security Strategy', p. 8. Retrieved from http://www.parliament.uk/documents/lords-committees/eu-sub-comf/ISS/cEUF061210ev2ISS.pdf

UK Home Office. (2017),). Impact Assessment # HO 0293. Retrieved from https://assets.publishing.service.gov.uk/government/uploads/system/uploads/attachment_data/file/742891/ECRIS-TCNImpactAssessment240918.pdf, retrieved. Accessed on January 23, 2019.

White Paper of the UK Government. *Legislating for the United Kingdom's Withdrawal from the European Union*, of March 30, 2017, Cm 9446.

EPRS – Papers of the European Parliament Research Service

Dumbrava, C., European information systems in the area of justice and home affairs: An overview, EPRS, May 2017.

Dumbrava, C., Interoperability of European information systems for border management and security, June 2017.

Dumbrava, C., Revision of the Schengen Information System for law enforcement, EPRS, February 2018.

Dumbrava, C., Use of the Schengen Information System for the return of illegally staying third-country nationals, EPRS, February 2018.

Gatto, A., Carmona, J., European Border and Coast Guard System, EPRS, October 2016.

Orav, A., Smart Borders: EU Entry/Exit System, EPRS, June 2017.

Radjenovic, A., European Travel Information and Authorisation System (ETIAS), EPRS, October 2017.

van Ballegooij, W., The cost of non-Schengen: Civil liberties, justice and home affairs aspects, EPRS, September 2016.

Voronova, S., Combating terrorism, EPRS, European Parliament, September 2017.

Media and Think-Tanks

Ilkka Salmi, INTCEN's Director CV. (2009). Retrieved from http://www.europal.europa.eu/meetdocs/2009_2014/documents/sede/dv/sede041011evsalmi_sede041011cvsalmi_en.pdf. Accessed on Novembe 4, 2018.

Independence Daily. (2016). *Why Brexit will enhance the UK's national security – Independence Daily*, 26 April. Retrieved from https://independencedaily.co.uk/brexit-will-enhance-uks-national-security/. Accessed on March 22, 2019.

Nomicos, G. (2015). European Union Intelligence Analysis Centre (INTCEN): Next stop to an Agency? Retrieved from http://rieas.gr/images/editorial/NomikosEUintelligence15.pdf. Accessed on January 20, 2019.

Statewatch. (2013). Secrecy reigns at the EU's Intelligence Analysis Centre. Retrieved from http://www.statewatch.org/analyses/no-223-eu-intcen.pdf. Accessed on January 14, 2019.

Statewatch. (2019). Disproportionate and discriminatory: The European Criminal Records Information System on Third-Country Nationals (ECRIS-TCN). Retrieved from http://www.statewatch.org/. Accessed on February 24, 2019.

van Buuren, J. (2009). *Secret Truth: The EU Joint Situation Centre*. Eurowatch. Retrieved from http://www.statewatch.org/news/2009/aug/SitCen2009.pdf. Accessed on November 3, 2014.

INDEX